How Big is Your Dream?

How 20 of My LinkedIn Friends Built Business Fame & Fortune

BY
RICK CHAVEZ

1

How Big is Your Dream?/Rick Chavez — 1st ed.
ISBN-13:978-1535313551
Library of Congress Control Number: 2016912126
CreateSpace Independent Publishing Platform, North Charleston, SC

CONTENTS

Dedication   Page   4

Gotta Work It!   Page   5

The Ones Who Do   Page 11

Start Small. Imagine Big! - Rick Chavez   Page 15

Create Tradition Overnight - Matt Levine   Page 31

My Kuleana - Patrick Landeza   Page 45

A Better Shot - Dr. Paul Kim   Page 55

Absorb it Like a Sponge - Ramon Sandoval   Page 61

Competitive Spirit - Andy Whatley   Page 71

Don't Kill Your Dreams - Rosiland Bivings   Page 81

Find the Right Attitudes - Ryan Vong   Page 91

Kudos to the Believers - Greg Jamison   Page 101

Nothing Beats That! - Ron Gonzales   Page 111

Do I Suck at It? - Tere Kampe   Page 121

We Were Good to Go - Tam O'Connor Fraser   Page 131

It Might Take 20 Years - Matthew Barnett   Page 141

Do It Anyway! - Steve Pavlina   Page 155

With Passion, Nothing is Difficult - Jeff Klein   Page 165

2005 was the Pit - Duffy Jennings   Page 175

Mechanic of the Body – Dr. Chris Colgin   Page 187

From the Bottom Up - Kurt Robinson   Page 197

Turn on the Switch - Sonny Melendrez   Page 205

Take That First Step - Ann Villapando-Chavez   Page 217

Do It Now!   Page 231

Partner with Rick Chavez   Page 233

DEDICATION

This book is dedicated to my wife, Ann, who has been my biggest supporter on this project and on every project I've ever done. No matter which new venture I've launched—book authoring and editing, Senior Living sales and marketing, video production or network marketing—Ann has been my #1 fan and motivator. She has the most loving heart of anyone I've ever known and deserves the best from God. I honor her with this book.

Thank you to my parents, Pete and Alicia Chavez, for how they raised me and for the countless sacrifices they made to provide for our family. They are the foundation for all the good in my life and I'll never be able to thank them enough. Nor should I forget my brother Robb Chavez and sister Suzy Crutchfield, both of whom I plan to spend more quality time with over the next few decades.

I've been blessed with five kids and I'm proud of them all. Ricky and Danny Chavez are my oldest sons, the kindest and gentlest young men you'll find. Charles, Macey and Joseph are my incredibly smart and talented step-kids. Hugs to all five of them for the love they share with me.

Most importantly, I dedicate this book to Jesus Christ, my Lord and Savior. Without His guidance and mercy, I would still be on the scrap heap of life. I serve one God and pray that He continues to lead me through the narrow gate.

"See, I am doing a new thing! Now it springs up; do you not perceive it? I am making a way in the wilderness and streams in the wasteland."
- Isaiah 43:19

GOTTA WORK IT!

Have you ever wondered why there are no television ads for Lamborghini? The answer is simple: because the people who can afford a Lamborghini don't waste their time watching television. For those of you who say you have the vision to become Entrepreneur of the Year, make a note of that. As million-dollar earner Eric Gryzbowski says, "To make your business successful, it's going to take work, work, work, work, work, work, work, work, work. Then you get paid."

KEEP KNOCKING

For many people around the world, Disneyland is a dream destination. Some families visit the *Happiest Place on Earth* three to four times per year. But how many of us would've heard of Disneyland if its founder hadn't taken persistent action to make his dream come true? Walt Disney went to 302 banks looking for a loan to finance his family theme park and he walked away from all 302 banks with nothing more than a firm handshake. But he never took 'No' as the final answer. He finally knocked on Door #303, which opened to the Bank of America, where he received the $17 million 'Yes' he had been searching for. "The way to get started is to quit talking and begin doing," said Disney.

Billionaire Isabel dos Santos is an Angolan investor who was named by Forbes as the richest female in Africa. She says that determination has virtually no limits; only the entrepreneur can decide whether or not the amount of work is worth it. "If you are hardworking and determined, you will make it and that's the bottom line," said dos Santos. "I don't believe in an easy way through."

Disney and dos Santos agree: get off the couch and do something to make your business idea happen!

FAILURE IS AN OPTION

True entrepreneurs are willing to risk everything, primarily their time and money, in pursuit of success. Everyone else in the job market is an employee who avoids personal risk and is satisfied with the safety of a salary with benefits and maybe a 401k or some stock options. Of course, the employee types still want to enjoy fine jewelry, cars, houses and the material things that signify great wealth. (See: credit card debt.)

Traditional employees expect to be paid regularly and many of them can, indeed, retire comfortably, but only if, and after, their employers cash in their chips. The bold employees eventually figure out that, unless they stake their own claim, they will never earn enough or keep enough to be financially independent for life.

Failure can be a scary notion, of course, but what if you succeed? Jeff Bezos, the founder of Amazon says, "I knew that if I failed I wouldn't regret that. But I knew the one thing I might regret is not trying." Amazon was up and running for years before finally making a profit but it's now one of the largest companies on the planet. Like the story of the *Tortoise and the Hare*, sometimes slow and steady really does win the race.

A DIFFERENT MINDSET

The entrepreneurial mindset can defy logic and sometimes their decisions ignore common sense but the properly motivated ones have clarity and their passion leads them to be successful. "Don't limit yourself," says Presidential candidate Donald Trump. "As long as you're going to be thinking anyway, think big."

The average 9-to-5 workers give up on their dreams far too easily and look at most new opportunities from the scared, overly cautious side of the street. Hugely successful entrepreneurs see opportunity and recognize possibilities and can judge realistic from unrealistic. Entrepreneurs might be partly insane but they typically work harder than the average Joe to drive their ideas to the marketplace.

WHAT'S YOUR MOTIVATION?

If you could actually count them, you'd discover that it takes millions of little decisions to go from Startup to Success. Tough times don't stop motivated entrepreneurs from success because each of them has a really strong *Why*. Everyone experiences tough times but it's a measure of your determination and dedication how you deal with and overcome these challenges. True entrepreneurs perceive windows of opportunities that ordinary folks don't. When it all boils down, it's the difference between believing that everyone owes you something versus believing that if you want something, you need to work to get it.

For the most part, *ordinary* people don't work to become rich. They wish it. They play the lottery or gamble on the stock market. They rely on Christmas bonuses or income tax refunds, and pray that their company 401k will outlast their retirement years. Some are content with their jobs, but most aren't. Most true entrepreneurs see a bigger picture and have a clear vision of where they want to go and the self-discipline to get there; they show empathy and inspire others and have an awareness of what can be done to re-shape the world.

Highly successful entrepreneurs adapt the world to their vision, not the other way around. They act fearlessly and are perfectly willing to change cultures to achieve their vision. Hong Kong billionaire Li Ka-Shing says that vision is a key ingredient to his success. "Without vision, you can't see to set goals or avoid unnecessary obstacles," says Ka-Shing. "Vision is perhaps our greatest strength. It has kept us alive to the power and continuity of thought through the centuries. It makes us peer into the future and lends shape to the unknown."

GAIN LEVERAGE

Successful entrepreneurs understand the power of leverage and teamwork. They think big, understand systems that create value, and place themselves into those systems effectively. They are smart enough to absorb the values of that system and recruit their intelligent friends to add to the culture. These entrepreneurs can identify massive holes in almost any industry and figure out how to create added value. They spend years attacking the opportunity, organizing people, recruiting and creating a winning culture. They create a Bible, so to speak, of values and ideas that attract other intelligent people. The difference at this level is knowing how to use leverage, one of the fundamental features of capitalism, to stimulate wealth creation.

CHANGE AND ADAPT

If you live in Detroit, Michigan where the auto plants have been shuttered, it's almost impossible to retire comfortably. But a century ago it was a great place to work and settle down. So, location, timing, industry and proximity does come into play. Online technology is hot now, but in the 1950s Texas oil wells were booming; in the 1990s we experienced the dotcom boom (and bust) in Silicon Valley. What will it be in the next decade? The ability to forecast the trends and hit the reset button in your mind is the key to success. There are many risks and uncertainties when starting a business but "The biggest risk is not taking any risks," says Facebook founder Mark Zuckerberg. "In a world that's changing really quickly, the only strategy that is guaranteed to fail is not taking risks."

STRUCTURE

Virgin founder Richard Branson says, "A business has to be involving, it has to be fun, and it has to exercise your creative instincts. In order to attract business and money, you need to offer something that's appealing."

If you watch *Shark Tank* on ABC, you'll see that most entrepreneurs don't actually have businesses, just products or ideas with no structure or form. They have no budget and no revenue. On the other hand, successful business owners do their homework and seek out long-term opportunities. Those with vision can see it, taste it and feel it and keep going until they reach their goals. "It's not the dreaming, it's the doing," said Mark Cuban, one of the most outspoken Sharks. "Being a total dreamer isn't going to make you rich. Ideally, you should balance the dreamer with the doer so you're both innovative and dedicated."

Entrepreneurs understand that if they want to be successful, they need to get rid of the employee mentality. They will never be envious of others making lots of money nor will they demand wealth redistribution to make things *fair*. They believe it's their own responsibility to prosper, not someone else's duty to make them rich. Most 9-to-5ers believe it's an employer's obligation to raise the tide that lifts their boat and those belief differences produce divergent wealth outcomes over time.

As the majority of 9-to-5 workers struggle to earn paychecks big enough to sustain their lifestyle or save enough for the end of their working days, one important piece of entrepreneurial advice to live by is, "You only make a change in life when you're sick and tired of being sick and tired."

How Big is Your Dream?

THE ONES WHO DO

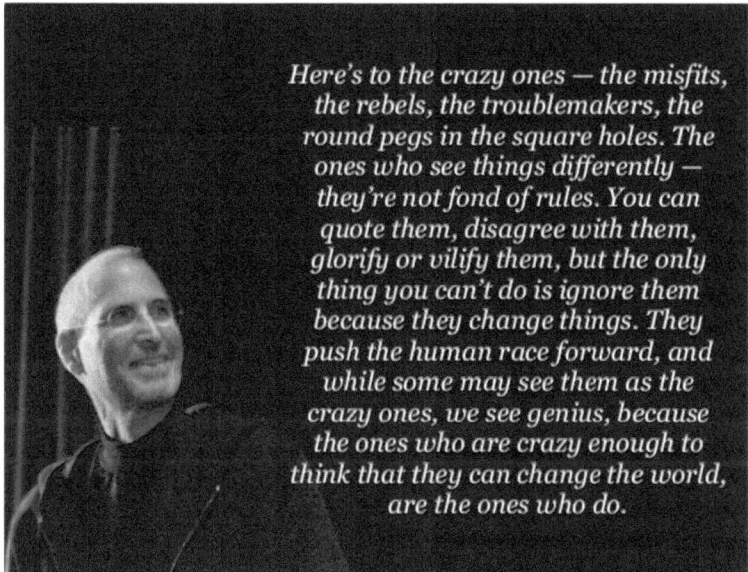

Here's to the crazy ones — the misfits, the rebels, the troublemakers, the round pegs in the square holes. The ones who see things differently — they're not fond of rules. You can quote them, disagree with them, glorify or vilify them, but the only thing you can't do is ignore them because they change things. They push the human race forward, and while some may see them as the crazy ones, we see genius, because the ones who are crazy enough to think that they can change the world, are the ones who do.

— **Steve Jobs, Apple**

MOST VALUABLE PROPERTY

There's a familiar story about a world famous motivational speaker who was invited to a ritzy Northern California hotel to train a huge group of energetic young executives and budding entrepreneurs. They were all so anxious to learn this man's secrets to success that they'd forked out $399 for the privilege.

As his seminar began, the man told his audience that on his way to the event he had driven past the most valuable plot of land on the entire planet. Since the hotel hosting the event was located deep in the heart of the wealthy Silicon Valley it didn't seem too far-fetched a statement. Many in the audience wondered to themselves where this plot of land might be located.

Was it the lush Hewlett Packard campus in Palo Alto?

How about the massive Google-plex in Mountain View?

Oh, maybe it was the new Apple Wheel in Cupertino!

If not, then it had to be Larry Ellison's 23-acre Japanese style ultra-mansion in Woodside.

Yes, the speaker said. Those places were quite pricey. But, No, none of them fit the description as the most valuable plot of land on the entire planet.

The correct answer, he said, was the cemetery off Highway 280.

Stunned silence from the audience.

The motivational superstar went on to explain that the cemetery is the most valuable plot of land on the planet because that's where an untold number of dreams, aspirations, inventions and world-changing ideas have been buried through the ages—never to be unveiled to the world—along with the people who were too scared, self-defeated, unmotivated, disillusioned or disorganized to pursue them.

ARE YOU STILL ALIVE?

As I approach my 60s, I see so many people dying at the age of 35. They won't be buried until they're about 85 but the will to live leaves them fifty years too soon. That sad truth is why I decided to write this book.

I've had more than my share of business failures that I attributed to the fault of others—a "guaranteed money back" project which was only guaranteed to take my money back to Pine Mountain Lake, a promising information product partnership that failed because of information *under*load, and a golf TV show that teed me up in front of a bankruptcy court judge. Considering those whoppers, it may be a good thing that so many of my other ideas and partnerships never even saw the light of day.

However, as I reflect now, all the failed projects were my own fault, especially the ones I didn't pursue. The ventures that I described failed because I didn't keep a reign on their progress, or my partners, as my effort, time and money were slowly and quietly siphoned away. The other ideas, the ones I didn't pursue, may have seemed too silly, difficult or costly at the time so they just got buried. I'm not saying that any of these ideas would've resulted in million dollar businesses, but who knows? Maybe I would've hit the jackpot if I'd been more alert. We'll never know.

So, thanks to the cemetery story, I've decided that no matter what life has thrown my way in the past, or the hurdles that will arise in the future, I am ultimately responsible for the consequences. That means that I have to unlock ALL my potential, not only for the ideas that are "guaranteed" to work or the ones that only help to ensure other peoples' fortunes. I need to take charge of my own work and savor the long-term results my efforts bring.

YOU CAN STILL DO IT!

There are major changes underway in the job market and they are already affecting everyone's career field. I'm sure there are many of you who are struggling with your long-term professional prospects and silently calculating whether you'll be able to save enough money to survive until retirement and beyond. It might be a layoff that has sidelined you or a demotion that has demoralized you or it just might be the drudgery of working in a job that you no longer love. Like me, you may have run into the not-so-transparent 50+ age barrier where young workers with low salary demands trump us old geezers despite our decades of valuable experience. I know how frustrating each of those scenarios can be because I've lived through them all.

But I'm not here to depress you. Just the opposite, I'm here to show you that there is life on the other side of a traditional job. I hope this turns into a life-changing book as I introduce you to a select group of my friends who all became successful either by starting a small business or by helping build a large company from scratch. I did a search on LinkedIn to see where some of my old friends were and found that many of them had left the uncertainties of the traditional 9-to-5 job market in pursuit of higher levels of career satisfaction, financial security, family bonding and spiritual wholeness.

At a certain point in each of their lives, they were encouraged by a mentor, a colleague, or a career advisor to follow their biggest dreams.

This is a collection of their inspiring stories.

"Start small. Imagine Big!"

RICK CHAVEZ
BROADCASTER / AUTHOR
RICK CHAVEZ MEDIA

Rick has enjoyed a successful career as a TV Sports anchor with NBC11, ABC7 and KRON4 in San Francisco. He's shared the screen with Hall of Fame athletes, Olympic champions and Silicon Valley executives. He was a business reporter for CNBC-Europe and trade show TV host for Cisco and Oracle, hosted a business radio show and won four Telly Awards for broadcast and production excellence. Recently, his content development skills have been targeted on the Small Business, Christian church and Senior Living markets where he's supervised, developed and produced professional print, web and broadcast content for consumer marketing and sales campaigns. He is the author of two books.

CROSS STREETS

Saturday mornings are made for sleeping in. But there's no rest for the weary ones who serve God's lost and forgotten. Miracles take place on Saturday mornings at 3 Crosses Christian Church in Castro Valley, California. That's when a dedicated band of volunteers rolls in to the side parking lot and gathers for Cross Streets ministry duty. They're organized to cook a hearty lunch for 50 or so, organize showers and haircuts, hand out toiletries and fresh socks, and offer prayer and encouragement to the homeless men and women in the surrounding community. My wife, Ann, and I have been plugged into Cross Streets for two years now and it's one of the most rewarding activities in our lives. It carries even more meaning because our kids get to join the effort and see what life is like on the other side. We are all humbled and blessed to be a part of the transformation in the lives of each person in need. We've made many friends among the Cross Streets guests and at times I've been blown away upon learning about their backgrounds. Some of these folks were highly educated and accomplished professionals who have, because of addictions, illnesses, family tragedies, bad financial decisions or misdirected life choices, become the faceless, homeless and "unclean" street people of the East Bay.

The fact is, no matter how financially secure we might think we are, each of us is all only one negative occurrence—a job loss, a car accident, a financial scam or divorce—away from being in the same food line as our Cross Streets brothers and sisters. I know, because it's still fresh in my mind how close I was to being one of their Tent City brethren on the cold and unforgiving streets of the Bay Area.

TV CAREER

My career choice and the time I spent as a media personality is still impressive to many of my friends and other sports fans I meet but it feels like the last forty years have gone by at lightning speed. After serving four years as a broadcaster with the American Forces Radio & TV Service (AFRTS) while stationed at Incirlik, Turkey, I left the Air Force to take a Sports anchoring position at KTSM-TV in my hometown of El Paso, Texas. My high school friends were excited, if a little bit envious, to see their still shy classmate on the air each night, delivering high school football scores, interviewing legendary UTEP basketball Coach Don Haskins, or broadcasting live from the annual Sun Bowl football classic. If I had stayed in El Paso all these years, I might have had a lifetime key to the city by now. But I thought I needed a bigger field to plow so I left for Corpus Christi, Texas and a job as an investigative reporter.

The I-Team job gave me the freedom to grow an ugly beard, wear sunglasses at night and snoop around other people's business like a mini-Geraldo Rivera but it just wasn't the real me. I wasn't comfortable sitting through overnight video stakeouts of slumlords or following the city water utilities truck on cold winter mornings to see if they were misreading the meters. The work was tedious and unrewarding and I knew right away that I had made a big career mistake. Fortunately, the weekend sports anchor was begging to go back to a weekday schedule (actually, he was lazy and wanted an easier job) and I was clamoring to breathe again so we got permission to do a job swap and I happily moved back to the "toy shop", a.k.a. the Sports Department.

I was back in my element, shooting football and basketball games with a Mt. Rushmore-sized RCA TK-76 camera, interviewing 17-year old Friday Night Heroes and connecting with a bevy of local coaches to

17

become the most trusted sports anchor in town. With things going so well, I figured Corpus Christi would be the final stop in my broadcasting career (key to the city?) but one day San Jose came calling.

San Jo-who?

NO, I DON'T KNOW THE WAY

This was still a few years before anyone other than Dionne Warwick or Cesar Chavez actually knew the way to San Jose; a time when the new Fairmont Hotel construction was displacing head shops and sticky-floored downtown theaters; when Silicon Valley was in the prep stages for the most amazing boom time since the gold rush; and when the only sharks in the Bay Area were patrolling for sea lion treats off the Farallon Islands.

I flew out from Texas to interview for KNTV's weekend Sports Anchor job and was wooed by General Manager Dick Fraim and News Director David Carrochi. Following our interview, they drove me up Highway 101 to Candlestick Park for a Dodgers-Giants game in the middle of May, which meant leaving before the 7th inning because Spring in San Francisco is like Winter in Antarctica. But I was impressed by the fact that I would be covering two major League Baseball teams (*major* in small letters because the Giants and Oakland A's were the laughingstock teams in their respective leagues), the Super Bowl champion San Francisco 49ers, Stanford, Cal and a host of other college, pro and Olympic caliber amateur athletes.

All that and much more came to pass as the years went along.

THE DYNASTY YEARS

I was on the scene when the Eddie DeBartolo-owned 49ers were in their heyday under legendary Coach Bill Walsh, then George Seifert. I

18

covered Monday Night Football battles, post-season grudge matches, record-breaking performances and the Joe Montana-Steve Young soap opera. I even shook #16's hand for the last time as he departed the Bay Area on not-so-friendly terms for Kansas City.

It was amazing how many future Hall of Famers I spoke to on a regular basis at 4949 Centennial Drive: Coach Walsh, Joe and Steve, Deion Sanders, Charles Haley, Ronnie Lott and Jerry Rice. Even though I grew up a Dallas Cowboys fans, I have to admit that these 49ers were among the all-time NFL greats. Over on the other side of the field, I saw the likes of Troy Aikman, Emmitt Smith and Michael Irvin as the Cowboys built their own dynasty in the early 1990s. Oh, and don't forget guys like Walter Payton, Reggie White and Eric Dickerson, Hall of Famers who did more than their share of damage to the home team on the damp Candlestick Park turf.

OCT. 17, 1989

Over on the baseball side, I witnessed the revival of the Giants and the A's, long-time doormats of their respective leagues. But with players like Will Clark, Robby Thompson and Candy Maldonado in the San Francisco lineup and the Bash Brothers in full destructive force in Oakland, the two teams restored luster to their faded reputations.

The reemergence of the two Bay Area franchises culminated with their Bay Bridge Series, or what eventually became the Earthquake World Series of 1989. I was in the freight elevator at 5:04pm, riding up with stadium workers and Chili Davis's family to the top deck when the temblor rocked the foundation of the stadium. Those fifteen seconds made Candlestick look like it was doing the wave and almost tongue-tied the normally unflappable Al Michaels. The natural disaster transformed us

19

from a sports crew to a news crew for the next ten days. When play finally resumed, the A's wrapped up the four-game sweep of the demoralized Giants but that October will always be remembered for the destructive images of the Marina District, the Bay Bridge and the Santa Cruz Mountains.

ALL-STAR MEMORIES

As with football, I got a chance to rub shoulders with baseball Hall of Famers. Willie Mays was a hoot at his first Spring Training as a Giants hitting coach in Arizona but Mike Schmidt and Reggie Jackson were always cold and surly. Rickey Henderson proclaimed himself the "greatest of all time" when he set the stolen base record but he always found time to banter with us on the field. I still remember with embarrassment asking Phil Niekro for his autograph as he came off the pitcher's mound one night in Oakland; it would soon click that it was against protocol to ask players to sign during a game. In today's parlance, "LOL!" I'll give Knucksie credit, though; he signed the ball for me with only a hint of hesitation. The late Kirby Puckett was another guy who would give you the courtesy, even if you were visiting media. He saved us with an impromptu live interview at the 1986 All-Star game in Houston when airport delays had cost us the chance to shoot pre-game interviews at the scheduled time. Kirby was truly a gentleman. Add the late Tony Gwynn to that list, along with Nolan Ryan.

WORST TO (ALMOST) FIRST

Unlike today, the Golden State Warriors were a troubled franchise when I first started covering the team. Joe Barry Carroll (Joe Barely Cares) carried a reputation for lackadaisical play, Sleepy Floyd usually lived up to his nickname, Ralph Sampson seemed to always fall short of expectations,

20

and Chris Washburn…need I go on? For a short time, the Warriors turned the corner with the Run TMC squad of Tim Hardaway, Mitch Richmond and Chris Mullin. They were the highest scoring team in the NBA during their best season but, sadly, Don Nelson's team couldn't play defense well enough to make a solid championship run. The rest of the seasons between then and their recent championship were more akin to watching a colony of termites chew up the slab foundation in your home.

ON THE FARM

There were many college teams that put together spectacular seasons, mainly the ones from Stanford, but on occasion teams from Cal, San Jose State and Santa Clara found themselves in national playoffs. Baseball, basketball, swimming, golf, and tennis were sports in which the Cardinal dominated. Tara VanDerveer's Stanford women, with Jennifer Azzi at the helm, won the NCAA Basketball title in 1990 while baseball took back-to-back crowns in 1987 and 1988 under Manager Mark Marquess.

CHOMPIN' AT THE BIT

As you might expect, one of the teams that I grew closest to was the San Jose Sharks, who played just four blocks away from my KNTV office. I was literally on the ground floor when the new arena was built and had lobbied on the air for San Jose voters to approve the bond measure. Mark Purdy of the San Jose Mercury-News was also a strong voice urging the NHL to expand to the Bay Area. I covered every one of the Sharks games from the time they played at the Cow Palace to their first two playoff seasons. They had been a horribly weak team, understandable for an expansion franchise, but when they turned it around and upset the Detroit Red Wings in their first playoff series, it was game on!

HIGHEST CALIBER ATHLETES

Individually, I was in position to interview everyone from Olympians Kristi Yamaguchi, Summer Sanders, and Carl Lewis, to Stanford golfer Tiger Woods, to heavyweight champ-to-be-again George Foreman. George was promoting his obscure comeback effort in Oakland, packing a load of more than 300 pounds. But the former champ displayed the look and the confidence that he would not only regain the title belt but also go on to become the King of the Grill.

There's a lot that I've left off this list, including my days covering San Jose State and Santa Clara athletics, Yosh Uchida's international Sumo Basho tournament in San Jose, the San Jose City College Track & Field meet that Bert Bonnano promoted, the celebrity-rich Pebble Beach golf tournament and countless one-off events that came to the Bay Area.

As I said, it was a career that many would give their right arm for.

SHIFTING GEARS

By the mid-1990s things were starting to become repetitive in the news industry so I decided to pursue corporate video production and to develop my own Radio and TV programming. I produced a number of marketing projects for Silicon Valley companies while keeping my on-air credentials current. I co-hosted Oracle Open World in San Diego and Apps World in New Orleans from an impressive $1 million studio newsroom and was the first to host a live webcast from the Netherlands for Cisco Systems. I also was the Silicon Valley reporter for CNBC-Europe and produced an award-winning story on Afghanistan's wartime economic recovery.

My business partner, Dan Cornell, and I got a chance to host a weekly talk show on BusinessRadio1220 in San Francisco where we had an awesome time interviewing dotcom founders and executives, most of whom, it turned out, were selling nothing more than vaporware. But talk radio with "Dan the Man" was a ton of fun while it lasted.

I still kept my hand in with the news stations, doing freelance work for ABC7 and KRON4 in The City. But the media world was rapidly morphing to a more tabloid style and viewership was headed downward, so the attractiveness of the business was wearing thin. Nearly ten years later, the caliber of local news is reflected in its dismal nightly viewership.

TOTAL GOLF (SCAM)

As I continued growing my freelance production company, one of my trusted business partners suddenly showed herself to be, shall we say, ethically challenged. I was the point man for a three-person team in the early 2000s whose goal was to produce a weekly golf show for KGO-TV. The 30-minute *Next on the Tee* program would feature a different course each episode, with tips from the pros, new equipment demonstrations and other tidbits of news that golfers wanted to know. Since I had an "in" at the station, we got a discount rate for airtime but it was still costly to buy 30 minutes of San Francisco TV time. I was to co-host with an LPGA teaching pro and handle all the pre- and post-production. The third partner was the wife of a prominent doctor who said she had all the connections to raise funding for the production and airtime. What a perfect trio!

The golf pro and I did our part, producing a season's worth of shows from places like La Quinta, Pebble Beach and Spyglass. I hired a cameraman and post-production person to edit the shows and their work was impeccable. But a funny thing happened on the way to golf stardom on KGO. Our money person had, indeed, tapped into a number of sources to raise the $250,000 we needed to pay our bills and make a little profit. But there was one slight problem: we couldn't locate her or the money because she had left the country with our funds (and, presumably, the funds from her husband's bank account. The poor guy was hosed worse than we were.)

Obviously, the golf pro didn't get paid and neither did I. However, since I was still in the TV industry and needed to maintain my reputation, I couldn't leave the crew members holding the bag so I paid them all off with my own savings (See: credit cards). The crew members never knew the difference because they were paid on time, in full. But for the next decade I was forced to rob Peter to pay Paul (not to mention Matthew, Mark, Luke and John) just to make ends meet. I became the master of the credit card shuffle and welcomed any and all 0% interest balance transfer offers that found their way into my mailbox.

As many of you have probably figured, that financial strategy is rarely endorsed in Money Magazine. You may have also discovered that the IRS does not like to be put on hold for taxes owed. And, by that time, the DotCom era had officially left the building so the radio show was off the list of money generating activities. That was a trifecta that squeezed, twisted and strangled my finances. What the heck, go ahead and throw in the divorce too, while we're at it.

WILL I EAT THIS WEEK?

So, during my time as a TV sportscaster in San Jose and San Francisco, I regularly interviewed Hall of Fame superstars like Ronnie Lott, Jerry Rice, and Joe Montana. As I went through those topsy-turvy times with my finances, though, I joked about eating Lotts of Rice and moving to Montana. I was broke, busted, and 100% disgusted. I had huge question marks surrounding all areas of my life—most of them centering around how to earn enough money to survive—but there were very few answers or people to turn to.

I got some much-needed relief in 2007 when I was hired as an Account Manager for Pure Matter, an award-winning San Jose branding agency led by Bryan Kramer and his wife, Courtney Smith. I still greatly appreciate the opportunity they provided me. Unfortunately, by 2008, the economy was kicking business owners in the shins and, since I was still relatively clueless as an agency guy, my price was not right anymore. "Rick Chavez, come on down! You've won a one-way ticket to the unemployment line!"

YEAR OF JUBILEE

They say that good things come to those who wait. God, was I tired of waiting! But, speaking of God, He turned out to be the one who had all the answers; I just hadn't been listening. Oh, I was looking for something. I tried Wayne Dyer and Anthony Robbins, visited the Buddhist church, and frequented the East-West Bookstore looking for something to fill the hole in my soul. Thankfully, God led me to cast my shadow on the front door of Jubilee Christian Center, a vibrant and welcoming non-denominational church that is still pastored by its founder Dick Bernal.

Some of the pastors, including Randy Estrada, later told me they recognized me from my TV days but none of them knew how far I'd fallen. So, each Sunday I'd go to the service and quietly fill my faith tank, then go home and read the Sunday papers at peace. Still no new friends yet, but I was beginning to see the Light at the end of the tunnel.

Six months or so into my Christian *career*, I was baptized and soon after that I was introduced to the Sports Ministry and its church softball program. I finally felt at home, playing a sport I loved, with guys who had my back, and I quickly grew into a leadership role on the diamond and in the church. My walk with God expanded when I signed up for Bible College (2011 Valedictorian), and joined the full-time staff as Senior Media Producer. My transformation was a case of iron sharpening iron as I became involved with various ministries that were mentored by strong men of faith.

3 CROSSES

Since then, I've moved on to 3 Crosses Church in Castro Valley, an amazing neighborhood church pastored by Dr. Larry Vold. Like Pastor Dick, Larry is a solid mentor with the inner strength it takes to handle the tough uppercuts that life likes to unload on us. It was Pastor Larry who officiated when Ann and I tied the knot at Skywest Golf Course on February 21, 2015. That day signified one more step away from a life of doubt and fear and one step closer to a future of imagination and possibilities. Ann and I are heavily involved in the Cross Streets homeless ministry, we host home Bible studies and stay as connected to the church as possible.

TO ALL THE JOBS I'VE LOVED BEFORE

Developing a personal relationship with God and marrying Ann have been the two most gratifying changes in my life, but moving from a traditional work style (as traditional as TV news can get) to freelance mode ranks third. Oh, I've ventured back into a regular work role on a couple of occasions, delving into the Senior Living business to learn as much as possible about a fascinating, but often poorly managed, industry. I've always returned to working independently because I like to own my time, have the flexibility to develop pet projects and choose who I work with.

Until 2015 I'd never considered network marketing. Most of the people I knew who were involved with network marketing were selling lotions and potions and real estate schemes that seemed sketchy at best. Many of these folks measure low on the integrity scale and register high on the BS meter but I guess they need to be that way in order to sell the stuff they're peddling. Having said that, the last place I thought you'd find me was in the network marketing world. But then Eric and Judy Rangel introduced World Ventures into our lives and the company has changed our income, our retirement goals and our perception of the network marketing industry forever.

This is not a sales pitch for World Ventures products so you don't need to raise your shields. But it is an endorsement of the people we've met in the organization and the integrity, training and teamwork that comes with the package. We are friends with top echelon earners like Tere and Mary Kampe, who are just as willing to roll up their sleeves as the freshest and hungriest newcomers. We know families like the Parhams, the Witts and the Mendozas whose lives have been changed. We see life returning to people's spirits as they discover that they don't need to be chained to the 9-to-5 desk anymore. The atmosphere and environment of WorldVentures has spurred Ann and I to even stronger faith and higher commitment to our God and to our earthly goals.

WEIGHT LOSS

One of those goals was to lose 30 pounds in 43 days. It sounds drastic, and it was, but the alternative was to keep bulking up on chips, sodas and popcorn until my belly burst out of my SuperExpando dress pants and "athletic" attire. One of the hazards of working from home is easy access to the kitchen and all the goodies that lurk there. That lurking was changing my physique from Charles Atlas (or thereabouts) to Charles Barkley. But Dr. Chris Colgin developed a plan for me to drop thirty pounds of fat by limiting myself to only 500 calories per day and drinking enough water to deplete San Francisco Bay. His goal was to see less of me more often and fewer than two months later the goal was achieved. I dropped from 222 pounds to 192 and have seen my metabolic age, my heart rate and my BMI drop drastically. On top of that, my arterial age has dropped to that of a 28-year old man, meaning the pipes inside my body are clean!

TIME TO GROW YOU!

This is the type of motivation that our new venture has sparked and it's caused a chain reaction of favor in our lives. Setting the right types of goals can do the same for you. It's critical to surround yourself with empowering messages and trustworthy people; avoid the negative voices and mediocre minds. If you decide to follow the lead of my friends in this book, I guarantee you'll face more business challenges than ever. But you'll eventually overcome them by eliminating ineffective habits and replacing them with productive ones that form the building blocks of a successful and well-balanced life.

Building your own business is an achievable feat—you don't need to possess any special skills or have a bankroll of money and you don't even need to have everything figured out. Learn as you go, be open to input and think and execute your plans like a determined entrepreneur.

Take risks and try new things that have the potential to position you for growth and wisdom. Gain knowledge wherever and whenever you can; read books, listen to podcasts or attend conferences to stay motivated and informed. It's time to leave the rat race to the rats.

KNOW YOUR PURPOSE

In 1818, a nine-year-old boy named Louis was sitting in his father's workshop outside of Paris. His dad was a harness maker and Louis loved watching him work. He even dreamed about being a harness maker just like his father. So his dad began teaching Louis how to cut the leather and punch the holes in the straps. But one day the hole-puncher flew out of Louis's hand and pierced his eye. This led to an infection that spread to his other eye and eventually caused him to be totally blind.

Years later, Louis was sitting in his garden when someone handed him a pine cone. As he ran his fingers over the ridges, an idea came to him. What if the blind could learn to read with their hands? So Louis Braille created an entire alphabet with raised dots, enabling millions of blind men and women to read to this very day.

Louis Braille's tragic loss of eyesight served a purpose but it took years of living with his blindness before he realized the reason for his pain. Just like him, our pain has a purpose as well. Maybe your career struggles or lack of motivation have led you to this book and to be inspired by the stories of how other entrepreneurs have faced and overcome similar challenges and disappointments. Maybe now it's time to know your purpose. Please let me know how your life changes.

Start small. Imagine BIG!

"We had to create tradition overnight."

MATT LEVINE
MANAGING DIRECTOR / CEO
SOURCE USA

It takes way more than a village to get a new sports franchise off the ground. It takes a marketing genius or two. Meet Matt Levine, a.k.a. Sports Marketing Genius. Matt was the guy I'd seek out to interview about the latest wrinkle in the emergence of the San Jose Sharks as the "World's Hockey Team." As they say, Matt has forgotten more about sports marketing than most people ever learn in a career. It's amazing how rapidly the professional sports business evolved from its Mom & Pop days to what is now a mega-billion dollar industry. Pay attention. Matt Levine was one of the pioneers.

EDGE 1.000

When Matt Levine was asked to host award-winning author Michael Lewis at a Commonwealth Club of California event, he told Lewis that he'd been principal of a company that developed the technology for the topic Lewis wrote about in *Money Ball*. Lewis replied that if he ever got around to writing a prequel it would feature a chapter on the company's system.

Turn the clock back more than three decades, when Levine was asked by the Haas family, the new owners of the Oakland A's, *'How can we increase our TV and radio ratings?'* His answer was they needed to give viewers more texture because baseball fans hunger for more statistical insight.

In the late 1970s, Levine met some of the founders of Sabermetrics, along with Dr. Richard Cramer, in Philadelphia. "When the opportunity to present this to the Oakland A's came up, I became the producer and co-founder of a new entity, Sports Team Analysis and Thinking System (STATS) with co-programmers Dr. Cramer and Dr. Steve Mann," said Levine. "We called it Edge 1.000 and launched it during spring training of 1981. We had a staff person in the broadcast booth with Bill King and Lon Simmons to collect, process and display the data."

The Edge 1.000 team needed hardware to make this happen so Levine introduced himself to the product manager for the Apple II. "I said we need hardware to develop what's going to be a very exciting sports industry application and I promise to get you five million dollars worth of promotional public relations value if we can pull this off," said Levine. "I knew it was going to be big. I'd spent the prior seven years talking to sports fans while running a successful consulting practice. I knew what fans wanted and, having interviewed more than 800,000 sports fans in all the major sports, I had the basis for believing it was going to be important."

The Yankees bought the system after the A's, and subsequently the Houston Astros and Chicago White Sox signed on. Levine's team began searching for investment capital and were on the brink of a major deal to leverage the application for NBC. Unfortunately, the proposal was abandoned because NBC chose not to invest in it. "Elias Sporting Bureau was threatened by us and said we were stepping on their turf," said Levine. "We figured we needed five or six teams to make it a going proposition. As we coached and trained the franchises how to collect, process and employ this data they kept on wanting more. So we had to keep investing in R&D but we didn't have the necessary capital. We wound up having to walk away from it and give it to Dr. Cramer who took it and tried on his own but wound up passing it on to another ownership. It went full circle before being reinvented with a syndication business model and becoming Stats LLC, now one of the most influential players in the world. It is multi-generations away from our original concept and it's a much better business now. Yet, the whole notion of collecting, organizing, geographically depicting and analyzing pitch-by-pitch information had been ours."

KNOW THE CONSUMER

Before becoming the San Jose Sharks Executive Vice President of Business Operations and Marketing, Levine's roots were in the consumer packaged goods world. He and his wife, Diane, fell in love with San Francisco and bought a home in the Bay Area, where Matt launched a food and beverage consulting practice, working primarily on marketing and new product development issues. "At the end of the NBA season, I was reading an L.A. Times article that listed the attendance for every team and the capacity for each of their arenas," said Levine. "I calculated that the league only sold 52% of its seats that season. It was obvious they had a marketing problem and suggested that there is a similarity between selling seats to an event and selling seats on an airline. They are both perishable commodities that have to be priced, promoted and packaged in similar ways. You can't sell it tomorrow if it spoils or the plane has already departed."

So, Levine began combining consumer and airline marketing concepts to determine how a team could sell more tickets. "In the summer of 1974, Golden State Warriors owner Franklin Meuli decided that he was going to hire a general manager named Dick Vertleib. I called Dick and told him I had written a one-pager indicating how I could help them. We spent two-and-a-half hours talking about the history of the NBA. No business. One thing led to another and that's how he became my first client in the sports world."

Levine didn't make enough money to cover his costs on that project but the work helped him understand the fan base. "Whether it was ticket sales, PR, community development or selling local sponsorships, I did research to help him understand the fans," said Levine. "That was my first opportunity and it translated into work with the Houston Rockets, which led to work with the Houston Astros, which led to work with the San Francisco Giants and it exploded from there."

In 1980 Sports Illustrated published a seven-part series that changed the world's view of the business of sports. "Ray Kennedy wrote two or three of the seven and I sent him a note that said many of the things he was writing about we were already doing with our clients," said Levine. "Six weeks later I got a call from Kennedy who said his editors had authorized him to do a sidebar on our company. So Ray came out and at

34

the end of the first full day he called up New York and said this is more than a sidebar. This is a full-page story!"

Kennedy stayed two-and-a-half days in November and by the end he said it had grown into a four-to-six page story. "I didn't hear from him so I called up in January," said Levine. "He says we have a problem. *'Because you've worked across all of these sports we don't know what time of year to run it. Have you done anything new since I saw you last?'* I said we had just finished a project for the New York Mets. So one thing led to another and in April of 1980 a six-page feature ran on my company. After that article ran I developed an acute appreciation for the value of public relations because the phone wouldn't stop ringing." That publicity led to a major relationship with the National Football League and through the 1980s Levine built a company that consulted with teams, leagues, arenas, stadia, racetracks and advertisers.

MEET THE GUNDS

During the late 1970s, Levine was introduced to the Gund family of Cleveland. At the same time, Mel Swig was posturing to move his California Golden Seals hockey team into a new downtown arena in San Francisco but he needed a temporary place to house the team. George Gund had a small sliver of ownership of the Seals and offered his arena in Richfield, Ohio. "They took the team to Cleveland and it laid an egg," recalls Levine. "Swig was viewed as a carpetbagger and was burned in effigy in downtown Cleveland. In the meantime, the Moscone Center in San Francisco eliminated the arena from consideration because they needed the space to expand the convention center. My former employer in New York was aware of the work I was doing and introduced me to the Gunds. I did a pivotal piece of work that led them to secure approval to

35

leave Cleveland and to merge with the struggling Minnesota North Stars. This type of transaction had never been consummated before and has never been done since."

The team worked hard to succeed in Minneapolis-St. Paul but Cleveland and Minnesota had merged as the two worst teams in hockey. Three years later, though, they parlayed high draft choices plus a bonus draft into a spot in the Stanley Cup finals. "But from a marketing point of view, they were never able to get it going," said Levine. "So the Gunds began eyeing the Bay Area as the largest market in the nation without a hockey team. Hockey had left the Bay Area in the mid-1970s and they felt the time was ripe to go back. The league was also looking to further open the West Coast. Wayne Gretzky had been part of a blockbuster trade to the L.A. Kings and the NHL wanted to give him company."

RUSH ORDER

The Gunds approached Levine again in late 1989. "Art Savage was the first CEO and employee number one," said Levine. "He said there was a Board of Governors meeting in March and, *'We want to go with a plan for moving to San Francisco this Fall. We're talking to people in San Jose who've just passed the bond issue for a new arena and we want to demonstrate that we're prepared and that means we need a plan that is imaginative and believable.'* They also needed a week-by-week countdown from March to September, a team name, logo, uniform designs, staffing plan and budget details."

The Gunds went to the meetings in March with the basics developed by Levine and his small project team but were turned down by the league. "The NHL said you can have an expansion team but we want to keep the other team in Minneapolis-St. Paul," said Levine. "But in return

36

for selling the team at a discount to Norman Green, we'll give you a call on a selection of their young players. So we had that special draft to take players from the North Stars who had fewer than twenty-five games of NHL experience. Arturs Irbe, Neil Wilkinson, Rob Zettler and Link Gaetz were formerly North Stars property."

Thus, San Jose was granted an expansion team to begin play in the Fall of 1991. The Gunds asked Levine if he would like to come onboard to implement his plans. "They made a very attractive offer and I took sixty days to wind my company down," said Levine. "I took a couple of key people with me and became the second employee, responsible for building the business and marketing side, the Sharks brand and their identity."

INSTANT TRADITION

This was a pretty special opportunity for the San Jose community and those who formed the foundation of the franchise but there was something very important missing. "We were coming into a market that didn't have any hockey tradition," reminded Levine. "There were people who had moved here from the northeast who may have brought some hockey interest but a lot of that enthusiasm had gone fallow. The NHL had a lousy TV contract and very few people knew who the better players and teams were. We were trying to build from scratch so we did a lot of research into crossover characteristics of people who might like hockey."

One of the foundational building blocks with the community was the Sharks & Parks program, which generated a major breakthrough into the future fan base. "We started knocking on doors of YMCAs and Boys & Girls Clubs trying to find out if there was any interest in hockey," said Levine. "At the Los Gatos Jewish Community Center the executive director said they had interest in floor and broom hockey. That became the basis for Sharks & Parks, which was targeted at young people playing in sneakers on gym floors and in driveways. Then we went to Franklin Sports and persuaded them to donate equipment and support. At its peak we had 55,000 Bay Area kids playing street hockey and, before you knew it, the league took it over, created Nike Street and bought our operating manual. I negotiated $75,000 worth of wholesale street hockey equipment in return for all of our intellectual property and then we redistributed it back into the market."

GEORGE GUND, WORLD TRAVELER

Levine calls Sharks owner George Gund the most peripatetic man he's ever known. Gund averaged 275 days per year traveling and had homes around the world, including Paris, Prague, New York City and San Francisco, plus a fishing villa in Washington. He had his own private plane and flew around the globe to pursue his interests in film, art and poetry and to promote hockey. Levine took a cue from Gund's life and set a goal for the Sharks to become the world's most popular hockey team. "Here's why," explains Levine. "If we could become popular and respected around the world and be featured in publications like the New York Times, The Wall Street Journal, The Boston Globe and Psychology Today, and TV networks like ESPN and CNN, that's going to come back into Santa Clara County and people are going to see that and say I want to be part of that. They may know nothing about hockey but they see that we're really creating community goodwill. Local publishers remembered going to New York City to pitch ad agencies and people would ask *'Where is San Jose again?'* But when the Sharks came along, the agencies stopped asking that question."

POWER PLAY

Like most professional sports leagues, the NHL was stuck in an old-fashioned mindset and the Sharks were double-daring the boys in New York with just about every step they took. "League headquarters said we'll be interested in seeing how you interpret Sharks because that's a pretty violent animal," said Levine. "So we came up with our graphics and opted for something that was appealing to adults and children, to teenagers and to pre-teens, to boys and to girls. It's because of our homework that we were able to come up with something that succeeded."

General Manager Jack Ferreira urged that one of the team colors be black but Levine knew they also needed a blue. But not just any blue. "I called buyers at J.C. Crew, Neiman Marcus, Bloomingdale's and L.L. Bean," said Levine, "as well as the leading hockey apparel licensee, Starter, and asked them which shade of blue would have legs for at least five years. Independently they all came back and said teal. There were twenty shades of teal, but Mary Keane, our director of merchandise operations, decided which shade to use."

The marketing team went to the league to show their wares and the league put up two instant roadblocks. "One was, *'We don't know how teal will look on TV'*, so they made us screen test the color," said Levine. "One night before a Rangers game at Madison Square Garden they had an employee put on a teal jersey and skate around with the cameras running to see how it looked against the ice. Then I got a letter from the president of CCM who said, *'You know, there are blues used throughout the sports world. The Rangers use a blue, St. Louis uses a blue, the Maple Leafs have a blue. You know you can make it much easier and we can get to market much faster if you just pick one of those blues.'* I said, I'm sorry, we're sticking with this. He says, *'Do you realize if you go with this teal we're going to create a brand new yarn?'* A couple of years later he was thanking me because of the way it exploded. We dared to be individualistic and to think that we understood what the market would embrace and we were right. Now, did we forecast that it would become as big as it did? No way. I would have been smoking something to think that would be as successful as it was."

REVEAL THE TEAL

When the Sharks launched their new uniforms Levine orchestrated an on-ice event at Vallco Fashion Park. The three hundred fans in the stands were those who who had submitted the name Sharks in the Name the Team sweepstakes. "I persuaded Gordie Howe to come to San Jose to lend his name to our introduction and to skate onto the ice with George Gund, wearing the home and road jerseys," said Levine. "There were eleven TV cameras there to cover the event and it wasn't just the locals. It was CNN, the major networks, ESPN and five local stations. The event made the sports news in the top fifty markets and newspapers coast-to-coast had syndicated photos of George, Gordie and the fans in our new jerseys."

THE SHARK TANK

Another area where the Sharks made a huge league-wide impact was with game staging. What should the fan experience at a Sharks game look like? "I brought in a former partner named Bob Brand, who came out of Hollywood," said Levine. "I had Bob literally invent what a Sharks game looked like. Bob developed the notion of the Sharks Head Tunnel. He had relationships with Disney and just as we were thinking about this, Disney spun off its float and rides department as a separate company. We became their first customer and they built the 22-foot high Sharks head. I had told Bob that I wanted something like The Baltimore Blast were doing in indoor soccer, bringing players through spewing CO_2. I wanted to do that and better."

Brand also developed the idea of the animated sharks flying through downtown San Jose and morphing into hockey players. He hired the laser company that also did the Pink Floyd concerts. "This company was curving laser beams," said Levine. "So Bob developed a script that allowed the crowd to see a laser animated hockey player skating around the arena. All of a sudden, a vicious shark appeared with the music of Jaws in the background, chasing and eating the opposing player."

REWRITING THE RULES

Levine said that, whenever the Sharks marketing team took a risk, management had the confidence that they were using good judgment while still pushing the envelope. Which reminded him of another light bulb idea that worked. "We picked a Rangers game because we knew that MSG Network would be broadcasting and that everyone could access their satellite feed," said Levine. "John Davidson and Hall of Famer Sam Rosen had their mics left on between periods and they were rewarded."

Rosen and Davidson were discussing how the Sharks were shaking up sports marketing and how the hockey world had never seen anything like it. "Look what they've done here at this old barn (the Cow Palace, original home of the Sharks)," the broadcasters commented. During all this, the Zamboni was doing its traditional ice resurfacing routine. "But then Zamboni abruptly changed course and faced the cameras while these guys were chatting," said Levine. "The Zamboni opens, CO_2 is spewing, and out comes our new mascot, S.J. Sharkie, to the music of Jaws.

41

Davidson and Rosen turn to the camera, *'Hey, are you getting this? Are you getting this?'* Rosen says *'This is phenomenal. God, these guys will do anything! They're so much fun.'* And that was the birthing of S.J. Sharkie."

KNOW YOUR MARKET

Levine says his insurance policy underlying all that marketing genius was his understanding of the customers and how they think. No team had as comprehensive a database of fan information as the Sharks. "We tested and refined our team name, logo and uniform designs once we had a direction," said Levine. "We got a lot of fan feedback but we took the lead. When it came to staging and getting people's attention, we used good judgment and reinvented ourselves and the game experience all the time. Heck, you go into New England and Red Sox nation, it doesn't get much deeper than that. It's embedded in the fabric of generation after generation after generation. We didn't have that; we were newborns. We didn't have a multi-generational following. We had to create it overnight and get every generation onboard...quickly!"

There was skepticism from Day One but inside the organization, there was a belief that they were pioneers embracing risk, with a willingness to do plenty of homework and make corrections as they went along. "Our PR agency and our artistic designers would say you give us good direction and then you give us freedom and listen in a way that makes us want to do even more," said Levine. "We managed creative resources like Bob Brand and Terry Smith who developed the original logo. We were the first and only franchise ever to have its own alphabet. Mike Blatt developed what we call Triangle Gothic, an alphabet built with triangles. The theme consistency paid off."

THE COOLEST LOGO

The level of detail that Levine and his team went to was unprecedented in the sports world. Most people don't know that even the triangle in the Sharks logo had very important meaning, which came via more diligent research. "I spoke to John McCosker from the Monterey Bay Aquarium," said Levine. "He's a prominent expert on the great white shark and associated with the California Academy of Science. I asked what he could tell me about sharks. We needed something regional so he said the area from Bodega Bay to the Farallon Islands to Monterey Bay is called the Red Triangle because it's the habitat for seven species of sharks. I said, Bingo, there's our triangle! Secondarily, if we wanted to be the Bay Area's team it also indicates where San Jose, San Francisco and Oakland are relative to one another geographically; it's a triangle."

THE WORLD'S TEAM

George Gund spent countless days and nights in Europe with General Manager Jack Ferreira, Head of Player Personnel Chuck Grillo and Scout Tim Burke. They turned the globe into their hunting ground for new players. "There are some war stories about those guys looking for talent and finding people in the middle of winter," said Levine. "We even signed the core of the old Soviet hockey team. We got Igor Larionov from Vancouver and Sergei Makarov from Calgary. The openness to looking for international talent was inspired by George. That was consistent with a major value of his."

A funny story occurred when Levine tagged the Sharks as "The World's Team". He figured it would be a great way to reach out to the international community living in the Bay Area. "So we hung the flags of the countries that our players came from," said Levine. "Then Art Savage got a letter from Harry Sinden, the general manager of the Boston Bruins. He said, *'Art I understand that your imaginative marketing people are celebrating your world ties and hanging their flags from the ceiling is very commendable. We're coming into town next and I want to make sure that you're not also singing all their national anthems because if you are we're going to stay in the locker room.'"*

25 YEARS LATER

Levine says the Sharks front office combined right and left brain activity, put it into the blender and out of it came unparalleled success. "When I started planning the 25th anniversary season," says Levine, "employees were so excited that what they helped create has endured as a brand and as a company. Many of them said this was the most important thing they'd accomplished in their lives. I've made more money doing other things, have gotten more publicity for doing other things, but being part of the ground floor of the Sharks is one of the most important things in my life."

"This is my *kuleana*, my responsibility."

PATRICK LANDEZA
MUSICIAN, COMPOSER, PRODUCER
LANDEZA PRESENTS

Slack key guitarist Patrick Landeza (born, he jokes, on The Island of Berkeley) is my newest role model when it comes to commitment, passion and servant leadership. He has performed at Carnegie Hall and made history in 2012 when he became the first mainland artist to nab a Na Hoku Hanohano award, which is the Hawaiian equivalent of a Grammy. Patrick is 100% dedicated to his music students at Moreau Catholic High School (they love when he brings in his Hawaiian *poke*) and his outreach takes him deep into the community, where he not only preaches the Bible, he also lives it.

MUSIC IN YOUR BLOOD?

When you listen to Patrick Kahakauwila Kamaholelani Landeza perform, you may get the impression that he was born with a silver slack key guitar in his hands. When you hear him perform *Inu I Ka Wai* or *Song for Uncle D*, you say this man is a natural from Day One, right? "Day one, no, but I have to say my house was surrounded by it," said Landeza. "It wasn't until high school when something just clicked. My brothers and I attended an all-boys high school and the one thing they regret not doing was music. I was the only one who took music and that's what launched the big interest and the drive. But it wasn't until my junior year when I started noticing all that slack key stuff and I'm like, Wow, there's something going on inside!"

DISCOVERING SLACK KEY

Landeza—whose heritage is Hawaiian, Filipino, Chinese and Irish—likes to joke that he grew up on the "Island of Berkeley", which you might guess was as far removed from Hawaiian music as you could get. That may have been true prior to the success of a musician/producer named George Winston. Winston produced recordings of Hawaiian slack-key guitarists for his own record label, Dancing Cat Records, including artists Keola Beamer, Sonny Chillingworth and Leonard Kwan. "Because of his Dancing Cat records and the slack key albums he was releasing during that time, Winston had built a huge fan base," said Landeza. "Two blocks away from my house there was a place called Freight and Salvage and that's where I saw a lot of the Hawaiian musicians. The masters would go to Freight and Salvage and there were all these fans and I'd ask myself, what's happening? This was amazing but at the time I was so young, I didn't understand it. World Music was a huge thing and those guys were doing it for a living. I'm like, wait a second, they're doing this and making money off it? That year my teacher and mentor, Maurice Harper, made us read a book called *Don't Sweat the Small Stuff*. In that book it asked, why are you going to work at a job that you don't like? Why not do something that you like and get paid for it? That just opened my eyes because I thought I had to be a specific thing, like a social worker. So, that just sparked it right there."

BACK STORY

Great performers like Landeza make their craft look easy, thanks to days, months and years of practice. Most of us can't even imagine what happens behind the scenes, but it takes hours and hours to become proficient in any endeavor, especially music. But Landeza says there's one factor that's even more critical than practice. "You have to find the teacher," he says. "It's so crazy when you see all these young guys popping up as YouTube sensations. When I started, I carried bags and drove in the snow. I negotiated things for the Uncles. I call my mentors and teachers the Uncles because I started from the bottom. After that they started to say, this boy is serious, and they would allow me to learn from them. Practice was the easy part, it was just finding the teachers. It was so funny because Hawaiian people were against me, since I'm not from Hawaii. They wouldn't sell my dance CDs on Hawaiian sites. I have a Hawaiian distributor, I have these Masters, I have special guests but they still wouldn't allow my CDs to be sold on their website. The number one website in Hawaii changed to a new owner and she would not sell my stuff because I'm from the Mainland. A lot of people were jealous. They sell my stuff now but if you Google an article titled 'Pat vs. the Volcano', it was the first time that I actually went a little militant; heavy duty article, Bro.

47

But I now have a mentor who's all for Hawaiian rights and he's been steering me towards who I am today as a Hawaiian born on the Mainland."

NO MORE BRAND X

When Landeza released his first CD people were impressed because the young Californian had worked with the great George Winston. As he catered to help pay for college, his reputation spread, which was good and bad. Most people thought he was just a good cook who played music. That's awesome, they said, he can cater and then he can play. The reality was, Landeza was ready to soar, both on the music and the business side. "As an up-and-comer, I was a natural at learning valuable business lessons from my Uncles," he said. "They said you can't play like us so you need to come up with your own brand. What's a brand? So they explained to me about the whole McDonald's thing. They said you have to develop a brand. That was so important to them and they had seen something in me."

One of his greatest mentors was Uncle Dennis Kamakahi who Landeza says would always inspire him and who was very much the rebel of Hawaiian music. "So my music began to evolve," he said. "I began to write more and then that was it, Bro. Of course, as a musician my brand changes and gets stronger and stronger as the years go by. I can play slack key enough to get by. I can entertain but when you see me on stage I'm just being who I am."

Building credibility became the top priority for Landeza and it finally began to click when the islanders saw him touring with the highly respected Uncles. "They were like, Oh, there something going on," he said. "These guys are trusting me and so all the other Masters below them also did. It's like martial arts, which has levels, and the second tier guys were now at the top. I befriended all of them and started producing their shows. I became a producer because the Uncles taught me how. So then I started negotiating because Hawaiians hate business. So now I'm the broker and the agent. Then I go on stage with them and it helps my brand as well, so it opened up doors for everybody."

BRUDDAH IZ

One of Hawaii's legendary performers was Israel Kaʻanoʻi Kamakawiwoʻole, better known as Bruddah Iz. The titanic sized man with the tiny ukulele had the biggest heart for the Islands and is still idolized nearly 20 years after his passing. No musician in his right mind would ever pass up the opportunity to open for Iz. Or would they? "I wasn't a professed brother but I lived in community in St. Mary's High School in 1998," said Landeza. "We were not allowed to play music. I couldn't do a concert but I got this phone call saying, *'We need you to be the MC and opener for Israel at the Marin Civic Center.'* I'm like, what? I'm freaking out. You've got to be kidding me. They're like, 'you're the only soloist, you're the only guy.' (I chose to be a soloist because I didn't want to deal with politics and I felt as if I practiced by myself I'd be better off. In other words, I would be a stronger musician.)

"So I had to ask permission from my Christian Brothers. Can I please play a concert? And he says, *'You know you're not allowed to play a concert'* and I said, I know, but it's for this guy named Israel. He says, *'OK, this is what I'll let you do. If you get me four tickets I'll let you go.'* He loved the show! It was the same thing with George Winston. The head Brother was a huge fan so every time Winston was in town he'd bring me into his office and ask, *'You don't happen to have any tickets do you?'* And I'd say, I got you Brother. You know, I was there for three years but that right there solidified my brand. Just by opening for Israel I began to

49

understand how this works. Play less, don't overdo yourself. Stop playing the restaurants, stop playing the bars and play more of the listening rooms and all the venues."

INNATE BUSINESS SENSE?

For some people, business comes natural. But that's not usually the case for musicians. They typically think with their creative right brain. But, for Landeza, the analytical left brain works just as effectively. "It's innate," he says. "I'm not going to say I'm from the 'hood-hood but you know I've worked in the 'hood. I worked for ten years in Oakland and I know the hustle. I never sold drugs but I've seen it around me. It's like the boba (Taiwanese bubble tea) for the kids. I've been giving away boba for two months and now they've asked me to sell it at one of their dances. The kids are hooked on this but you know where that money is going? It's going to help our music ministry buy ukuleles. So it's planting the seeds, looking at your market and seeing how you can serve your market. When we sell the boba it will make an impact on the program."

Once he "got it", nearly every business venture that Landeza has gotten involved with has become a winner. Although, in one case, he had to rework his strategy to make the Aunties happy. "I started making bracelets and the big ladies were mad because I'm not making bracelets big enough for them. Holy crap, I think I got something! You see what I mean? But those items are also helping the catering and the poke business. Costco started selling poke and I'm like, holy mackerel, I can do that! I just post on social media and these people are at my house. You can see my brand here and everywhere I go."

TALKING STORY

It's a rich Hawaiian tradition to "talk story". Every picture tells a story and in traditional Hawaiian culture, so does every song, dance, item of clothing and even food. Music is a vessel for a story, whether that story is an oral history, an experience, or a look at where you came from. It's all about keeping tradition alive. "My masters told me that slack key playing is only fifty percent," said Landeza. "So, Uncle what do you mean? He says, *'When you're on stage it's only 50 percent. The other 50 is your ability to tell stories.'* When I was invited to perform at the Native Americans Story Telling Conference, I asked why? I'm a musician. What do you want me to do? So he goes, *'Do what you do; tell the story, sing the song.'* OK, I do what I do, fifteen minutes I'm out, and an elder comes up to me and the first thing he says, *'You, son, are a Storyteller.'* No, I'm a musician. He's like, *'No, you are a storyteller.'* It's so important to get the story. When you're teaching and you're making the classroom come alive, the story is everything. Emotion to me is everything."

Another perfect example of talking story occurred at Brigham Young University where Landeza was scheduled to perform with two other 'cats' who looked a little rough around the edges. "So I go up to the boys and they're all tattooed out and all they do is play slack key," he recounted. "They are harmless but they look like thugs. They go, Pat, you've got to go on first, take care of it. I got fifteen minutes and in that time I not only need to get my story across, I also have to get the whole slack key thing across. By the end of that set the head of the event came back to me and started crying, I mean, he was just in tears. He was like, I can just listen to you all night. They told the two others to keep it short or else everyone was going to leave but nobody left. There was a thousand people still in that house. So storytelling is so important."

MENTORS

Landeza's father, Danny, was outgoing and community-minded and he and his wife, Frances, mentored their kids about the importance of helping others in the community first. In fact, Landeza's lengthy and spirited service was recognized in 2006 when he became the youngest recipient of the Kapalakiko Aloha Spirit Award. Outside the home, Landeza ran into an assortment of mentors, including his school teachers and others who exerted great influence in his life. Decades later, he's now mentoring students at the high school level, many of whom are at the most impressionable stage of life. "My mentors were awesome," he said. "You steered the wrong way and they guided you back. They led by example and steered you the right way. Today, I'm proud of my students who are doing well and the ones who chose to have some sort of career in music. Let those be examples and inspire the others, that's my thing. I don't go out and tell people I've played at Carnegie Hall; they can find that out. I try to tell my students, whether they are rap artists or opera folks, just remain humble and your humility will make you a celebrity; I promise you. If you're a YouTuber and you have 125,000 hits in a week, you can be as arrogant as you want on YouTube but when you go on stage you've got to be down to earth. These folks who chose that industry have done well for themselves but I'm always mentoring them."

LIFT SOMEBODY UP

Obviously, Landeza makes a living making other people smile and he's perfected the ability to tell stories and entertain even the most hardened concert goer. But how about on those days when he's not feeling up to par or something in his life has gone south for the moment? What keeps the man at the head of the parade going? "When I'm feeling down I just remember my teachers and the great times we had on the road," he says. "All these new cats coming in, you put yourself on YouTube and you're a celebrity. I didn't have YouTube. I remember saving my money so I could send out a 350-person mailing list from George Winston. I borrowed his addresses and told people I need you to put me in your clubs. A couple of folks were so hardcore, they kept saying you need to pay your dues. Make sure you pay your dues. We're talking about Cyril Pahinui; we're talking legends of slack key guitar and of World Music who are being honored by The Grammys. These guys are huge and they get very emotional because they knew I took bullets for all of them. Watch the movie trailer on my new website; when you hear the whole story, it's crazy, but I'm hoping to inspire others. Young folks come up to me and they're scared to talk to me and I can remember that when I was younger. I'm like, come here boy, don't be afraid. You just got to do what you do and play your music and give them words of encouragement. That's what needs to happen."

KULEANA

There are so many talent competitions these days, it'll make your head spin. Not just the high profile network TV shows but also school and community talent shows. Every musician is looking for that big break and Landeza has advice for them. "You have to be resilient," he says. "It's so funny, I met somebody who plays Mexican music with his nephews and they're doing good things. He didn't know me from Adam but I tell him just don't give up. When people Google me it might not sink in at that moment but maybe a month down the line they freak out. Everyone's like, dude, do you know who this guy is? You just can't give up, you have to be resilient, and when people shoot you down you just have to get back up. I almost gave up but I was destined to do this. This is my *kuleana*; in Hawaiian, that's responsibility. This is my responsibility. My ancestors already determined it. There are so many times I wanted to quit but *kuleana* told me that I needed to continue. This is more cultural than it is a business but like that book said, I'm getting paid for something that I love to do. I'm affecting lives and I can make a difference just by my music."

SPIRIT OF ALOHA

People always say that the wife of a musician is either a saint or crazy. Landeza confirms the fact that his wife, Jennifer, is the former and says that, as a successful musician, you need to have that understanding significant other. "When I was younger, I had an opportunity from George Winston to tour with Cyril Pahinui and Dennis Kamakahi as their manager and we knew where this was going," he said. "I was a Vice Principal and on a Principal track, but I'm getting offered by the Uncles to take a two-year break to tour with them. My wife said, *'I want you to do your music. I want you to do this now while you're young so you don't regret it in the future.'* That's who my wife has been throughout. She used to handle my schedule and all that but with the children she delegated it. So the inspiration comes from her and from our four children (and one on the way). But also very importantly, my parents. I can walk into any Bay Area Hawaiian event because they were so important to the Hawaiian community. There's the spirit of Aloha in everything that I do, from the music to the jewelry, to the jams, to the children's book, the CDs and the poke. That's who I am, that's me all together. That's the brand; most importantly that's who I am as a person and we are as a family."

"I have a better shot than anybody I know."

DR. PAUL KIM
MANAGING PARTNER
PARAKLETOS VENTURES

Dr. Paul Kim is a straight shooter when it comes to...well, everything. He never pulls punches when it comes to demanding quality and it shows in the success he's enjoyed as a lawyer, pastor and venture capitalist. I met Dr. Kim when I became Media Director at Jubilee Christian Center. He is the Chief Executive Elder of the 35-year old church and has lessons on how to gain business leverage and set up the foundation for success without sacrificing your integrity.

BUILDING A BASE

Dr. Paul Kim was blessed with an entrepreneur mindset and, while already distinguished as the first bilingual Korean lawyer in Silicon Valley, during the last four decades he's also added the roles of pastor and venture capitalist to his *curriculum vitae*.

While Dr. Kim was still attending Hastings Law School at the University of California-Berkeley, a huge legal firm passionately courted him to take an assignment in Chicago for two to three years in order to orchestrate the launch of a South Korean office. After much thought, he opted to accept a much less glamorous job at a Christian summer camp in Korea, serving as a youth pastor under the venerable Pastor Yonggi Cho. "I became a lawyer in 1983 and immediately set aside money to start investing. I met Dr. Cho in 1986 and the following year I started working for him," said Dr. Kim. "I used to travel more than 250,000 miles per year with him, flying all over the world to do Christian missions work and manage television crusades. I ran his TV broadcast and was a co-host for more than 10 years. So, during that time, my plate was full as a volunteer pastor, co-host and global TV director."

CHRISTIAN TV

After he founded the Kim Law Firm, he started a San Jose-based television company that featured broadcast sermons by Dr. Cho, who was well on his way to building the biggest Christian church in the world; today nearly one million people call Yoido Full Gospel Church their spiritual home. "I had the opportunity to join that large law firm but if I had, then I wouldn't have started the TV show," said Dr. Kim, "nor would I have had the time and the mobility to travel with Dr. Cho."

Dr. Kim obtained the broadcast license from KTSF-TV, a postage stamp-sized multilingual station on the San Francisco Peninsula. Dr. Cho's weekly program was aired throughout Northern California and became one of the most popular shows on the station. "Dr. Cho's people would send me the tapes after they aired the program in Korea," said Dr. Kim. "We would edit it, drop in local commercials and then show it in the Bay Area. It eventually went international via satellite but I never made a lot of money on the program because the advertising revenue was tiny. It turned out to be more of a contribution to the local community but I got built-in advertising for my law firm and other benefits from the broadcasting venture."

At that time Dr. Kim was only 26 years old but his high public profile paved the way to the presidency of the Korean Community Center where he was able to secure funding from the United Way and the City of San Jose to purchase food and other necessities for those in need.

Dr. Kim continued to boost his professional standing and by the end of the 1980s he had become the president of the Silicon Valley Korean Chamber of Commerce and President of the Silicon Valley Korean-American Association. "I was doing all of this pro bono community work partly because of that TV thing," said Dr. Kim, "but it didn't hurt my legal business, as you could imagine."

FRONT PAGE NEWS

Within the first four months after opening his law practice, Dr. Kim found it necessary to hire two extra lawyers, mainly because of a negligence case that wound up on the front page of Bay Area newspapers and on the 11:00 local newscasts. The case centered on a man who had died mysteriously in his hotel room in South San Jose. The authorities took the body from the scene but failed to investigate the cause of death and allowed the hotel manager to rent the room right away. "Two Korean guys rented the room the next night and one died in his sleep. It turned out to be carbon monoxide poisoning from the gas heater," said Dr. Kim. "I had an open-and-shut case of negligence against the City of San Jose and the hotel owners for allowing the room to be rented without investigating why the first guy had died. The proper thing to do would have been to conduct an autopsy and tape the place up so that nobody could rent that room. I was on the front page of the San Jose Metro and KGO-TV put me on television for a whole week."

BUILDING A PORTFOLIO

As Dr. Kim continued to parlay his legal expertise into connections and his connections into lucrative investment opportunities, his entrepreneurial chops began to reveal themselves. Kim was the initial investor in Silicon Image, the company that invented High Definition Multimedia Input (HDMI) technology. Silicon Image was formed in 1999 and remained a standalone until 2015 when the firm merged with Lattice Semiconductor. "Every television set in the world, whether it be in Africa or China, now has HDMI because it's the new technology standard," said Dr. Kim. "We went public in 1999 but I invested in the company before anyone was on board. Almost all of my companies are global companies. We may create a company that is U.S.-headquartered, but all of the activities and my engineers are generally outside of America."

Dr. Kim prides himself and Parakletos Ventures on being extremely market observant with the ability to forecast what will happen at least three to five years into the future. "Intel used to make DRAM, but the Koreans took that business and now own 90% of it," said Dr. Kim. "LCD displays used to be U.S. military technology, but the Japanese picked that up. The Japanese took the LCD market and the Koreans took the DRAM business. One is trying to get bigger (LCD) and one is trying to get smaller (DRAM). This market was made possible because American companies were not going to invest seven billion dollars in a manufacturing plant and risk not making money."

Dr. Kim and his team also made a prescient forecast that the LCD business would eventually migrate to Korea so he deftly invested in a display technology company. "We know Korea, we know how to handle Korea, we know how to sell in Korea and all our engineers are in Korea," said Dr. Kim.

At one time in the not-too-distant past, Korea owned a measly 2% market share in the LCD industry but today Korean companies produce nearly 100% of the high end displays in the world. "They occupy about 65% of the entire LCD business globally," said Dr. Kim. "But they occupy 100% of the high end. So we were right in predicting that LCD was going to be a major industry in Korea and we knew that we were going to be close to the customers."

Dr. Kim made similar forecasts with GCT Semiconductor, his flagship company, where he serves as Chairman of the Board. GCT Semiconductor specializes in LCD chip sets. "When I started GCT fifteen years ago, Korea had practically zero market penetration," said Dr. Kim. "Today Samsung is the largest handset manufacturer in the world, Apple is second and LG is third. Because I'm Korean, and because I know all the orders that are placed by these companies, I'm able to sell into that market and know the customer better. I know their niches and their needs before other people do. If it works right, I have a better shot at selling than almost anybody I know."

THE LEGACY CONTINUES

Dr. Kim, who now wears an additional hat as Chief Executive Elder at Jubilee Christian Center in San Jose, California, is proud of his entrepreneurial ways and says that all four of his children also share that gift. "Monkey see monkey do," he jokes. "But there is an enormous amount of hard work and persistence necessary to succeed. I helped raise a family but still partnered with Dr. Cho to do ministry and managed a law firm at the same time. God has blessed me enough that, even though I was not around ten to fifteen days a month for a long period of time, my kids are all devout Christians. They all went to very prestigious schools and have amazing jobs. But it takes a lot of work and a lot of persistence. You know there are many failures so you have to not get discouraged. I use the Word of God, of course, to keep me on track."

"I absorbed it like a sponge."

RAMON SANDOVAL

FOUNDER

VINO LATINO USA

When I put out a call for entrepreneurs to feature in my book, the first response came from Ramon Sandoval. He says he struggles with marketing his emerging company but he had the right instinct when he jumped onboard this project. Ramon is a dedicated entrepreneur who has parlayed a new love for wine into a budding business. He knows he doesn't have all the answers but he's partnered with many people who do and when you hear his sincerity about growing his business with the right principles, you'll discover the essence of a true entrepreneur's dream.

EARLY NAPA

The Napa Valley's rich winemaking history began about a decade before the California Gold Rush of 1849. Wild grapes grew in abundance but it wasn't until settler George Calvert Yount moseyed through the Valley and saw the area's potential for cultivating wine grapes. Yount built his homestead and in 1839 became the first person to plant Napa Valley grapes. It wasn't very long before other pioneers including John Patchett and Hamilton Walker Crabb helped introduce the first *vitis vinifera* grapes to the area. By 1889 business was booming with more than 140 wineries in full-scale operation.

The tremendous expansion was brought to a halt in 1920, though, when Congress enacted the Prohibition law. Vineyards and wineries were abandoned for more than a decade with only a handful of wineries continuing to operate. When Prohibition was repealed in 1933, Napa Valley's wine industry began to recover slowly. In 1944, seven vintners formed the Napa Valley Vintners trade association, which has grown to more than 525 wineries today. That obviously means *'Thar's gold in them there grapes!'*

MARQUEZ BROTHERS

It seems like a bit of a stretch to follow that historical narrative with an overview of Marquez Brothers, a family owned food distributor in the San Francisco Bay Area that's well-known for its authentic Mexican style dairy products. Under the brand name El Mexicano, they sell more than one thousand popular grocery items. The link between Napa Valley wine and Marquez Brothers is a gentleman named Ramon Sandoval, who worked for El Mexicano and now stakes his claim in the wine industry. He was enjoying a very successful career with the company and looked to be satisfied for the long haul. "I was Regional Sales Manager and they'd send me to put fires out at stores throughout Northern California," said Sandoval. "I'd travel all the way up to Ukiah. When the numbers were low they'd send me out to 'spank' the sales team and show them how to expand our product line with proper placement to give the customers a better chance to appreciate our brand."

As he made his weekly drives through the Napa Valley to handle his duties, everything about his job seemed fine on the surface. Sandoval would make routine calls on a handful of stores and discuss sales strategies with management. Little did he know at the time but his entrepreneurial and personal future lay directly outside of his front windshield. "Driving through the vines was so soothing and I was mentally at peace. None of that hustle and bustle," he said.

FUTURE PROSPECT

One meeting in particular caused Sandoval to increase the frequency of his trips to canvass the Napa and Sonoma regions. In 2011, he met his future wife, Becky Tyner, at a Starbucks and learned that she owned Small Lot Wine Tours, a small, family-owned company dedicated to small, family-owned wineries. Not long after they met, Becky asked him to go wine tasting with her. "I told her my story, that I didn't drink wine," said Sandoval. "But the education she provided about the aroma, the swirling of the glass, the whole wine business and the logistics of it was fascinating to me. Wow, this is pretty cool stuff! I would never have thought to look at it that way. So we started to go wine tasting and I was having a lot of fun. This was good stuff, smelling the aromas and tasting the different flavors of the Valley, where a cabernet tastes different when it comes from a different peak of the mountain. As she explained these things to me, I absorbed it all like a sponge."

VINO LATINO USA

Soon after meeting Becky, Sandoval took the plunge into the wine industry and founded Vino Latino USA with a group of family, friends and other wine connoisseurs. Soon he realized that, to be as successful as possible, he needed to get face-to-face with the consumer. "Wine tasting is intimidating because people think it's a prestigious thing, that only those with money should do it," said Sandoval. "That's how I felt going in. When I started wine tasting I was very shy, just observing everything that was coming at me. It can be intimidating. In my regular 9-to-5 job, I had stability and was making good money. To walk away from all that gave me a scary feeling. Did I make the right choice? It went from a sure paycheck every two weeks to it's all about me now."

Sandoval began to do in-home wine tastings billed as Vino with Amigos, which has since become a giant hit throughout the Northern California circuit. "I go to people's homes and educate them about wine, recounting my experience as a novice and reminding them that it takes time to build a certain palate," says Sandoval. "You have to start somewhere, preferably in their home where they feel comfortable enough to ask questions. That's how I started building my wine club. I buy wine at wholesale and sell it at retail in their homes." Sandoval originally began his new business venture in San Jose and San Francisco but he's recently expanded to Sacramento and Orange County. With the concept taking firm hold in the midst of a discerning audience, he will soon commission a Vino with Amigos representative in Los Angeles.

Sandoval says it has helped in many ways that he was not originally a wine drinker because he has a new and fresh appreciation for the grapes. "It was never something I considered," he said. "I tried it 20 years ago but it was a very cheap, horrible tasting, mass produced wine. I was like, 'Oh, my God, what is this, where's the beer?' Over the years I'd go to someone's home and they'd come out carrying a bottle like a baby, *'Oh, look what I have. It's a 2000 from France and this and that.'* I would just ask, 'Where is your beer?' In my mind I said I tried wine already and I didn't like it."

SOMETHING'S AMISS

As Sandoval toured more of the Napa Valley region, he found the wineries impressive and the settings beautiful, but something in particular stood out like a sore thumb to him. He noticed that there weren't any Latinos in the tasting room, only in the fields and buried in the back end of the operation. He noticed the workers in the cellars and saw that they assisted winemakers but were not inside the tasting room where most of the fun happens. "I started talking to them to try to get their story and when I would ask, 'Do you drink wine?' they'd say, *'Yeah, I drink wine. My cousin makes this wine.'* I was like, wow, this is something I would like to partake in and learn more from the Latino winemakers," said Sandoval. "My wife, who's American, is a real wine educated geek, and I asked if she knew any other Latino winemakers. *'Well, there's a few out here,'* she said. As it turns out, they were right in front of me all along."

The majority of the Latino winemakers in the Napa Valley have relocated to California from Mexico. "My parents moved here from Mexico," said Sandoval. "My dad crossed the border when he was sixteen and worked in many places in California. I'm first generation Mexican-

American, my first language was Spanish, and I remember seeing the dedication that they had. They just knew that they wanted to make a better life for themselves."

INDUSTRY GIANTS

As he conducted his research, Sandoval met an impressive array of local winemakers in person. Among them was Cesar Toxqui, a winemaker who hails from Mexico City. Toxque actually started a brick building business as an enterprising young man. When he was 14 his uncle gave him the opportunity to move up to Ukiah where he was introduced to the wine business by a classmate whose family owned a winery. He also met Gustavo Brambila, from Jalisco, Mexico, the winemaker and owner of Gustavo Wines; Reynaldo Robledo, from Michoacán, Mexico, the founder of the Robledo Family Winery; Everardo Robledo, the winemaker and one of seven sons who are involved in the family winery; Mario Bazan, who has worked for iconic vineyards such as Joseph Phelps and Robert Mondavi. Bazan was in charge of the famous Opus One Winery and To Kalon Vineyard for 16 years before moving on to the prestigious Stags Leap Vineyard; and David DeSante, who is the winemaker at Mario Bazan Cellars.

Gustavo Brambila was featured in the 2008 movie, Bottle Shock, based on a true story that chronicles the events leading up to the famous 'Judgement of Paris' wine tastings. Mr. Robledo's father joined the bracero programs back in the 1940s at the peak of World War II. He came to California from Mexico to work in the fields. His son Reynaldo Robledo worked side-by-side in the hot sun with his father and chose to stay when the elder returned to Mexico. Reynaldo began working as a picker and eventually got involved enough in the wine business that he started a vineyard management company and invested in what is now real estate heaven—astronomically valuable property in Napa Valley. He went to France to study and has since built a very successful business for his family. "I think they are the largest Latino immigrant-owned properties in the Valley," said Sandoval. "They own land in Lake County and now in Sonoma, Napa and Mendocino Counties. All their wines are made on their own property so they don't outsource any grapes. Presidents have visited their establishment and their wines have been featured at White House functions. Their story is just amazing and it all started after arriving here as immigrants."

Sandoval asked Becky to take him to meet Gustavo Brambila. "I wanted to throw around this crazy idea that I had to feature their brand in a wine club," he said. Sandoval spoke to Señor Brambila and asked for his blessing, but he was extremely careful and respectful, not wanting to step on anybody's toes. "Gustavo said, *'Ramon, that is a fascinating idea. What you want to do is help other Latino winemakers get their brand out to showcase their wine to the world.'"*

SHOWCASING THE BEST

Since Mexico is racked with so much poverty, a good number of their country's finest winemakers have moved to the Napa Valley and worked their way up the ladder. "I want everybody to know that the Napa community is great with the Latinos," said Sandoval. "They support them and give them opportunities to climb up the ladder to become winemakers. Unfortunately, when a winemaker gets to that point, I feel it's the name on the bottle that receives all the recognition. There are a few people who will ask, *'Who's the winemaker?'* but I would say 90-percent of the people just look at the label."

When it comes to showcasing the best selections around the world, Vino Latino USA features a growing assortment of Latino winemakers who all appreciate him opening doors to new clients. "Yeah, they say, *'Oh, my God, Ramon's doing it. We're selling to him wholesale but he's out there telling our story in front of people we're never going to get in front of.'* I'm telling their story in a bottle and hopefully they get future clients right then and there who will buy their wines from me. So it's a win-win for them and they are heavily appreciative of what I'm doing. Now I have people contacting me from all over. I'm starting to get my name out there," said Sandoval.

Many of the 'new money' wine connoisseurs are Silicon Valley technology people who are recently minted multimillionaires with ever expanding portfolios. The potential for big money is there for Sandoval and his new venture. "Obviously it's a great concept," he says. "We have been to more than 250 wine tastings and are now doing a lot of team building events with Google. We're attracting many of the younger generation who are more into wine, including second and third generation Latinos who are more professional and love the product because it's an artisan wine, a hand-crafted wine."

HIDDEN GEM

There is an interesting story that emerged from those professional events which has opened up a potential gold mine for Sandoval. "The first thing my clients would ask is, *'Hey, Ramon do you have a sweet wine, like a Moscato?'* Over and over people would ask me. So I went to all my winery friends and said, 'Hey, you guys want a cash cow to make some extra money? People are asking for the Moscato.' But they told me I was crazy. *'We are not Moscato makers, we are Cab makers, Rioja makers,*

68

Syrah makers, Zin makers. We're not Moscato makers.' So I looked at my wife and said I had to do it," said Sandoval. "I found another fabulous wine maker in Mendocino County and told them I'd like to partner on a project to make a Moscato. We did just that and it's a rock star! It's the number one seller wherever we take it. It's a light, sweet wine called Vino S Vida. We are being creative and people love that!"

Despite the meteoric success of Vino S Vida, Sandoval and his wife are forced to slowly ramp up their business because they don't yet have the expertise to reach the masses. Marketing a startup in this industry is difficult and the workload often stretches the couple beyond their limits. "It's overwhelming because we are trying to grow," says Sandoval. "We're still a startup and people say they want to invest in our company. I say, 'I can't take your check because you don't know anything about wine, and I'm just learning, so I'll just waste your money.' I'm a born-again Christian; I believe in God and I don't want to do the wrong things to people or their money. What I need is someone who knows what they're doing. I'll be honest with you, we could use marketing help."

IT TAKES FAITH

Sandoval urges all of you true entrepreneurs to go with your heart. Never take 'No' for an answer, just follow your vision. "If you get doors closed on you and you don't like that or you can't handle it, I'd guess that entrepreneurship is not for you," he says. "If you cannot take 'No' for an answer then it's not for you, because it is hard. You just have to keep rising."

Sandoval reminds us that the entrepreneur is the walking brand and logo of the company, so you've got to represent yourself well. "My wife is very supportive when there are things that I'm not happy with, or during those many times when you want to quit. *'Ramon, we're going to get through it. Don't quit, we've come too far.'* It's important to have a support system at home," says Sandoval.

For Sandoval and his wife, the number one support system is their Christian faith. "God has guided me through a lot," he says. "He put something in my lap that I ask, 'Why did you do this?' I question it but have faith that He knows I am the person to succeed at what I'm doing. So I strongly believe every day and thank Him for giving me this opportunity and guiding me through it. Jesus, He's the Man!"

"We went after the marketplace."

ANDY WHATLEY
DIRECTOR OF SALES
NEXSTAR BROADCASTING

In the DotCom days of the late '90s, I co-hosted a weekly radio show in San Francisco. My radio partner and I found Program Director Andy Whatley to be one of the most energetic media pros we'd ever worked with. Andy showcased our program with a great time slot, worked out the best financial deals and gave us leeway to develop our experimental radio format. We interviewed a few startup winners but they were mostly vaporware peddlers. Andy kept us on track with high energy, integrity, big market sales knowledge and years of valuable experience.

BROADCAST dot WHAT?

Andy Whatley doesn't hide his admiration for the Silicon Valley giants who changed the world with their ideas. Apple? Check. Google? Check. Facebook? Check. There is one particular business idea that he wasn't necessarily fond of at the time, but which went on to land a huge fortune for the entrepreneur. "You know Broadcast.com was a great idea, but what's even greater is that it caught the attention of Mark Cuban," said Whatley. "He didn't make a lot of money running Broadcast.com but he made a lot of money from selling it. The thought behind it was, if I give free streaming away to radio stations, I can get them to give me a feed of their local college sport and then I can sell that online to an audience that will pay for it. Cuban made it all possible with his first concept of streaming media in the college sports marketplace. Lightning struck at the right moment and he had something Yahoo thought would grow. Ask them today if they would buy it again, if they knew what they know now and I think the answer is No."

SINK YOUR FOUNDATION

On occasion, Whatley will run into a friend selling a far-fetched idea that has a very minimal chance for success. He gives them advice that he wants all entrepreneurs to take to heart. "I've told lots of friends to be honest with themselves about the level of resources they need and how long they'll need to stay afloat to make their entrepreneurial dream a reality," warns Whatley. "If you're honest with yourself, your chances of success are greatly improved. If you don't fill all those check boxes you'll have problems from day one. My friend in New York is always working on the next big dream but he can't pay this month's rent. Hey, if you can't pay the rent then your entrepreneurial dream is not going to be a reality. You've got to be able to feed and clothe yourself, pay your utilities, keep your bills paid and still do it, and that means you've got to have a job, at least part-time, that provides a predictable stream of income. Get that first and then start your business."

DAVID VS. GOLIATH

Whatley first became an entrepreneur when he obtained a license for a new FM station in South Texas. It was so low power that it didn't even cover the whole market. "We went into it knowing that we didn't have an adequate signal to cover the Rio Grande Valley," said Whatley. "We were a little Class A 3000 watt station but we were able to convince ourselves that we wouldn't fail; even though we didn't have a competitive signal we had a competitive spirit and we went after the marketplace. Guess what happened? We went on the air as a country music station. Our main competitor was operated by a media company that owned primarily Spanish stations. We knew that if we could beat up on them a little bit, they would go away and switch their format to Spanish."

Whatley's team performed as if they owned the biggest signal on the planet and convinced others with the quality of their programming. "We started doing well just because of our brash and spirited attitude," said Whatley. "What eventually happened was a station with a 100-thousand watt signal went on the market for a low price because it was not making money. We bought it, moved the country format to the 100-thousand watt signal and the next thing you know we're now the most competitive radio station in the market! All these years later it's owned by iHeart Media. Today it's called KTEX but we made that station a huge success story, sold it for millions of dollars and made money. It was really just our belief that we couldn't be stopped. Maybe it was being ignorant and not knowing that we could fail."

Whatley's team was anchored by four aggressive salespeople who followed him south from a station in El Paso. Along with his partner, they formed a crew of six very good salesmen. "One of the cool things about advertising is that it is pure salesmanship," said Whatley. "It is driven totally by your ability to get a business to invest in your airtime. We had six great sellers on the street who came back with a bunch of contracts on sheer will and pure salesmanship. That's what drove our success. The world changed for us because we got the chance to buy that other station with a low down payment. We moved the format from a little signal to a big one, spun off the little signal for a half-million bucks and ended up with a 100-thousand watt radio station. Today KTEX remains one of the dominant radio stations in that market place. We positioned it right from the very beginning and owned the country music segment in that market and nobody can touch them. I wish I still owned it."

RADIO OR WEB?

Broadcast radio listening has been in a serious decline for years. Pandora has more than twice the audience of all of the radio stations owned by Clear Channel, CBS, Cumulus, Entercom and the next seven broadcasting companies combined. Add to that tens of millions listening to iTunes radio, Google Play, Spotify, XBox Music, Rhapsody and other audio startups, not to mention SiriusXM and the explosive growth of streaming on smart phones, and it's clear that broadcast radio's monopoly has reached its end.

That sea change became apparent to Whatley in his 40s, when he joined Bay Area startup Kiptronic. "I was the oldest guy on staff for the very first time in my life," he said. "Everybody was twenty-something including our CEO/Founder. What I noticed immediately, moving from a traditional radio environment to a technology based one, was how much smarter the people who worked there were than those who were in my previous environment. This company was full of very young, smart people and it really made me step up. Suddenly I didn't feel like I was the smartest guy in the room anymore and my arrogance couldn't drive the bus. I thought, these guys are really smart so I need to step up, I need to focus, I need to read, I need to study, I need to bring my game up."

Whatley says the key to their success was that none of the young entrepreneurs thought they could fail. Or if they did, they were willing to take the risk. "Of course this is something that comes with youth," he said. "At 60 I ski a lot different than I would at 25. It's just a natural thing when you're young. You feel like, hey I've got plenty of time to correct. If I waste all my money or lose all my money, I'll just start over. Obviously when you get older you think about that and you become more risk averse than the average bear. At a certain age you can't afford to fail and your appetite for risk changes. So I highly recommend that you don't go work for the big corporate monster. Get out there and do what you want to do because who knows what you could achieve?"

ADAPTATION

As you might have gathered, Whatley is fascinated with digital media consumption, especially the change that live streaming has made in the face of traditional broadcast radio. "I'm fascinated by all of the advertising technology that surrounds it," he said. "I also find programmatic ad buying fascinating because it removes a seller and a buyer and automates the transaction. It does what Google did with

AdWords, when they first discovered that, instead of having to know ten thousand big customers, you could service millions and millions of little customers. Google is doing it that way with the local businesses, using an automated system for placing advertising. There's no shipment involved. They put in their credit card, enter their Ad Words, hit their keywords, submit and decide how much they want to spend and they're done."

Whatley says that audio media companies, broadcast or Internet, will gain a strong competitive advantage when they create irresistible original content. "It's especially urgent that broadcasters create dazzling content exclusive to the online platform; otherwise, they'll be fishing where there are no fish," he said.

CLOSE TO THE ACTION

Andy and his wife have settled for good in El Paso, half a state away from Austin, which is considered the digital media and music mecca of America. Think South by Southwest. "Austin went international and then became the new music center for all forms of music," said Whatley. "It's now a magnet that attracts a very deep level of creative types who want to be in that space. They want to be where it's all happening. Austin is to music what Silicon Valley is to technology. Silicon Valley is clearly headquarters and it's a magnet for every technologically driven entrepreneur who wants to be where the action is. They want to be close to Sand Hill Road where the money comes from and around other business builders who have cutting edge ideas. They are all over there because they want to be in that scene just like San Francisco was in the hippie era— everybody wants to be where it's happening. That's Austin for the creative music types."

GREAT MENTORS

Whatley has enjoyed and appreciated the benefits of mentoring throughout his career. There are too many individuals to name them all but at least one gentleman stands out from the crowd. "In the broadcast industry, it was John Douglas, who was actually a rocket scientist by vocation but a broadcaster by avocation," he said. "He was a guy who never thought he could fail. He started off by putting a television station on the air when he knew nothing about the industry. But he learned how to buy and sell and he would buy radio stations and sell them for multiple valuations at a time when you could still do that. He took advantage of the moment and built an empire worth millions of dollars. He never could operate or manage a station to save his life. It just wasn't his thing, and he would be the first to tell you. That can't be done today because of the limitations and valuations of radio stations."

EDUCATION CHANGES

As the years go by, more people from foreign countries are making an impact on the American entrepreneurial system and Whatley thinks the world has already caught up to us in terms of innovation and business building. "In terms of who's turning out the next Bill Gates, I'm not sure if the U.S. will have anything to do with that," he says. "I think we're going to see them come out of Asia. You look at scores of our high school and college graduates and we do not dominate the space anymore. I don't think that we are ahead, as we would like to think we are, but I don't think we're carrying a hand basket either; there are many great minds in the United States. I think we're going to continue to be one of the leading countries, but why do we have to be number one anyway? What's that all about? Is that 'mine's bigger than yours' kind of thinking? I don't believe that's important. It's about quality not quantity. We don't need to be number one."

Speaking of education, how can the American educational system better serve the coming generations who likely will need to be entrepreneurial to survive? "At some level they have to become incubators and not just buy the notion that the only value in education is the traditional," says Whatley. "The list goes on and on of entrepreneurs who didn't go to college: Steve Jobs, Bill Gates and Larry Ellison didn't graduate from college. These are all incredible entrepreneurs who never followed the traditional education path. I think educators ought to get out of this trap of thinking their way is the only way."

For years, Google wouldn't hire a person who had less than a 3.1 GPA. That rule no longer exists but Whatley says it hampered the company's growth for a number of years. "They ended up with a herd mentality where everybody thought the same way, were not risk takers and were not entrepreneurs," he said. "They were all from the same gene pool, so to speak. What they found is that it wasn't giving them that entrepreneurial spirit that would keep their organization growing creatively. They were systematically excluding those people. Google finally realized that was a big mistake because a lot of guys who didn't finish school are pretty bright and come up with incredible ideas and have incredible drive. I think you can get too caught up in the traditional mindset of education and having a bachelor's degree or a masters or a PhD. Not that those are bad things; more education is always better. However, if you do it at the exclusion of people who might not go that path you're cutting out some of the brightest minds. That's why schools need to be incubators and not just factories that churn out people with a paper degree. You better hire people who can take risks and a lot of times the college factory is pumping out these very bright young minds that aren't necessarily the same kind of risk takers that Gates, Jobs and Ellison were. It's so funny, all three of those companies require someone with a degree and they were founded by somebody who didn't have one."

WHAT'S NEXT?

As he ponders the future, Whatley is always on the lookout for the next great investment opportunity. "Around the Bay Area there is a chain of coffee kiosks called Caffino," he said. "The right location will fascinate me because it's a business that does $30,000 a month; that's $1,000 a day with $12,000 profit every month. I want to find that key location where the traffic comes from two ways. That's as far from technology as you can get but it's got my attention."

Whatley reminds us all that 'what's old is new'—including the drive and motivation to go the distance in business. "The difference between success and failure is to never give up," he said. "The people who are successful are the ones who keep at it one day longer, one hour longer, one year longer than the ones who quit and failed."

"You can't allow people to kill your dreams."

ROSILAND BIVINGS
PRINCIPAL
BIVINGS COMMUNICATIONS GROUP

As a Sports anchor, I covered the Pebble Beach golf tournament each year. All the major celebrities were there, from Tiger Woods to Clint Eastwood, Phil Mickelson and Bill Murray. I'd also meet Rosiland Bivings, who truly stood out among the primarily white male media. Not only was she a woman, Rosiland was an African-American woman, doing player interviews on the practice green. Our friendship grew until she left the Bay Area to care for her Mom but recently I discovered that she's resurrected her annual women's golf tournament. I'm happy to know that her entrepreneurial persistence continues.

TEED OFF

Almost half of the businesswomen who responded to a recent survey said that their exclusion from social networks was the #1 hurdle to reaching their career goals. Golf was targeted as a common example, which raises two obvious questions: are women being purposely excluded or are they excluding themselves? The answers are Yes and Yes.

IBM is one of three major corporate sponsors of The Masters Tournament at Augusta National, which many consider the most prestigious golf club in America. As a long-standing courtesy, the CEO of IBM has historically been granted automatic membership to the club but the guidelines were (not so) mysteriously changed when current CEO Virginia Rometty entered the picture. Rometty, who was named one of the Top 100 Most Influential People in the World by Time Magazine in 2012, was denied membership to the club until public pressure finally forced Augusta to open its doors to her in 2014.

Not every story of exclusion is that dramatic but it may indicate why professional women still feel ostracized from the good ol' boys golf network, primarily because of intimidation and the fear of embarrassment. Most women assume that the men who play in corporate outings are good golfers but that's far from the truth. Many women also assume that the men who play golf do not want to share the course with women. There are some cavemen exceptions, but in general, that's also wrong. Women who exclude themselves from corporate golf events are missing out on many business benefits, the biggest among them the opportunity to develop relationships and to be where high-level decisions are made. The time is ripe for women to seize the opportunity that golf affords.

YOU PLAY GOLF?

Having said that, meet Rosiland Bivings, who says that being a woman of color and an entrepreneur has its pluses and its minuses. Often, people in the business world would ask, *'You play?'* Yeah, I play," said Bivings. "That was usually the first question out of their mouth and it made me keep my game because it was actually my credibility. Golf opened a lot of doors and put me in a position to be in places where I would not have normally been. I have been fortunate enough to be around some of the top executives and tournament sponsors simply because I was in the golf business."

Bivings has taken advantage of her standing, getting to know people in high places and piggybacking on their influence to help open doors. She was once a guest on the Golf Channel, has written books and been invited to be a corporate event speaker. Her business has been helped by the fact that she's not a shy person. "You need to have the audience and the fact that I had a TV show really boosted my visibility in circles that I would not have ever had a link into," says Bivings. "I have benefited quite a bit from the fact that I play golf and that's why I wish I had known this sooner. I didn't know you could make a living doing this so I actually came to the game late. But the fact that I've been in sales and marketing for most of my life put me in position to sell things and sell myself, or to promote my events or products. That has shown me many doors that I would have never been able to come to, let alone open on my own."

TIME TO STEP UP

Even in today's world, Bivings says the business world does not really care for women but they don't realize it until they get deeply entrenched in the environment. "It's geared for you to be very aggressive, to be very forward in your presentation, to be very demanding, to be very thorough," she says. "I've been through this and you need to actually be better than most men in the marketplace. I think that women feel, because they are a woman-owned business, certain doors are going to automatically open up. Nope, it's not true. You really have to earn that status. You have to establish yourself as someone who's credible, somebody who's willing to take the high risk. A lot of that has to do with the way women are socialized. We are not really socialized to go into business on our own or we deal strictly with women in our business endeavors."

Bivings says that more women now see that they have the ability and capabilities to go into mainstream business. Unfortunately, many times it takes a man to bring them into those venues where a woman needs to have a thick skin. "Men are very direct," she says. "Women tend to hem and haw around and don't like to say No. They want you to like them. I'm not offended and don't take things personal because I've done more business with men than I have with women. I think women are finally realizing that it's OK to be tough and it's OK to say No. It's OK to put yourself out there and say I'm going after this, this is what I want to do. Regardless of what you tell me, I'm going to do it."

ON THE JOB TRAINING

For the longest time, Bivings had wanted to be an entrepreneur but so many people, including her closest family and friends, questioned her goals. Who's ever done that? Who do you know? "I don't know but I'll figure it out," she told her critics. "I look back at my experience in the golf business. I had no idea how to do it so I called everyone. I met the late Betty Hicks, one of the founders of the Ladies Professional Golf Association (LPGA), Master LPGA Teaching Pro Kit Carver and LPGA

Hall of Famer Juli Inkster. All these ladies told me stories and were encouraging. I would go to them for advice and they'd let me make my own mistakes. But I turned something I did not know how, but wanted to do, into something that was successful and is still my passion. It made me a great living."

Bivings created an event in the early 2000's called the Women's Corporate Open and hosted it for five years. The economy stalled and the event was forced to shut down but it's been reborn as the Bay Area Business Women's Classic. "I love the game of golf and I really wish I had discovered a lot earlier that you could actually make a living and do business playing golf," she said.

Golf remains one of her passions but anyone who knows what an event planner does understands that organizing a tournament involves a lot of work. It's quite an endeavor and it takes at least six months to put together. "People don't just show up and play," says Bivings. "Planning means deciding what kind of course you're going to play, what type of golfers you're going to have, and how to make it a fun event. Then there's finding sponsors, prizes, deciding what kind of contests you're going to have and getting the publicity for it. Golfers are pretty temperamental and you get a variety of players, from the very experienced to the novices. I try to make it fun, challenging and competitive all at the same time so everybody has a good time doing it."

Finding a course is the hardest part because the wrong venue will stress people out and make them never want to return. "You want them to walk away having at least a decent experience with their round of golf," she said. "On the day of the event, of course, you need to have everything ready so that it's well worth the players' effort and time and they walk away feeling great and talking about the next one."

NETWORKING

When corporate golfers play in her events, Bivings tries to make the day even more productive by getting the players to network. This is how men have been doing business for years and she says women are finally taking advantage of this kind of opportunity. "I always tell the story about the first Women's Corporate Open," said Bivings. "I introduced a woman who was a Vice President of one of the major airlines to a friend who was a sales director for a small woman-owned bakery. I put them in the same group for a reason, so that they could meet each other and see if there was anything they could do together besides play golf. Three months later they came to me after they'd signed a deal for the bakery company to provide all the breakfast food for this major airline. This is how guys, and now women, do business."

ON THE AIR

Considering the majesty of Pebble Beach, Spyglass, The Olympic Club and Half Moon Bay, golf is a big deal in the San Francisco Bay Area. But there has been a dearth of local golf TV programming that showcases the up-and-coming players and the amazing venues. Bivings produced and hosted a show for local cable TV with that in mind. "I did more than fifty shows and I remember the first show I did," she recalls. "After reviewing the tape I went, 'Oh no, I can't do this. This is not right.' But that helped me to develop my teleprompter skills and writing copy for my show and the way I wanted things to look. I was in Mountain View one day and a guy walked up to me and said *'You're the golf lady'* and I said yes and he said, *'I watch you on television and we even watch your reruns. '*"

The ability to present on camera helped Bivings develop the poise that's needed to present to an audience. "It was actually a door opener for me when people knew that I was on television and it really elevated my abilities and my position in the golf industry," she said. "The television show was absolutely the best thing that I did. It really helped me."

ROLE MODELS

The person whom Rosiland admires the most and who was the biggest mentor in her life was her mother, Josephine Bivings. "My mother owned Josephine's Beauty Shop for 45 years," she recalls. "She went to Beauty College and decided that she wanted to have her own salon. Now we're taking about the '60s and she didn't know how she was going to do that but she knew this is what she wanted. She went to work for another hair salon for a year to learn the business. Then, after she figured out all the things she needed to know, she opened up her own shop. I watched that as a youngster growing up. My mother decided she wanted her own money, she wanted her own clientele, she wanted her own hours, she wanted to run her own operation. She was the biggest influence in my life."

Later in her own business life, Rosiland was pushed around a little bit but she survived and thrived. "My goal was to be president of a company in Silicon Valley and I had a mentor who saw that in me, who guided me along until I hit that glass ceiling," she said. "I realized the only way I was going to be president of a company was to be president of my own. There are lots of women out there whom I've watched along the way. Women with small businesses who made a difference and proved that you didn't have to be a giant multi-million dollar company, but you could run your own shop, own your own successful business by just doing what you love. I can look at Anne Cribbs who started the American Basketball League and worked tirelessly to put that league together. It set the stage for the WNBA. LaDoris Cordell, a good friend of mine in San Jose, is the police auditor. Great inspiration, great spirit and really looking out for women, protecting them and encouraging them. There are just so many whom I could name but the number one on that list is my mother."

LIFT SOMEONE UP

Mentoring in schools is now one of the more satisfying activities of her life. "I don't do the traditional mentoring of youngsters because too often you get that same 'Do good in school, do this or that.' I ask them to be audacious," says Bivings. "I ask them to see what they want and don't let anybody say you can't do it. People around you can be your biggest dream killers. Sometimes their discouragement tells you things. There were two young ladies who told me they wanted to open a hair salon but didn't want to go to college. So I said OK, here's my questions for you. First of all you've got to have a beauty license and how are you going to know how to price your products? You don't need to go to four years of college but go to community college, learn how a business operates, find people who are in that business. They said that every woman in their family had told them they were stupid and that they would never make it. All they needed was somebody to say, 'OK you can do this.' I love doing that kind of stuff. I gave them my card and said when you open your salon I want to be the first customer."

Bivings reminds kids that many world changers made it in spite of people telling them they couldn't because they had imagination. "To be an entrepreneur you have to be different and you have to have a mindset that says failure is OK," she said. "Thomas Edison created ten thousand light bulbs before he got the right one, so he figured out ten thousand ways not to do it. So you have to be different and you have to be persistent and you can't allow people to kill your dreams."

SURVIVE AND THRIVE

The final tip from Bivings is that entrepreneurs must continue refining their individual skills day after day after day. "From speaking, to presentation skills, to marketing skills, to personal skills; understanding what you need to do and where you need to be because timing is very important," she says. "There are ups and downs to being an entrepreneur and you have to be able to survive both. Do your research and have people around you who are encouraging. Don't let anybody fool you into thinking you can just go out there and start your business. Make the investment in personal development and training materials. It's not just a freebie. It's an investment in your life. I've done that throughout my entrepreneurial life to make sure that I am always at my best."

"Find the right talent and attitudes."

RYAN VONG
FOUNDER / CEO
DIGITAL PI

When I first met Ryan Vong, he was a wide-eyed young man who was absorbing every tidbit of information about the budding Internet. I was a freelance media producer and I could see that Ryan's web team had spirit and talent and they only lacked experience. Years later we reunited at Pure Matter, where he helped upgrade an already successful team to higher levels of production. Two decades into our friendship, Ryan now has an MBA and is the CEO of his own company, hurtling towards a prosperous future. You'll be hearing a lot about Ryan and I'm proud to say you heard it here first.

ONE-MAN BAND

It's been nearly a decade since Ryan Vong decided to create his own company. He'd seen many businesses come and go over the years and he'd worked under a number of management styles so he wanted his own venture to reflect his values and work ethic. "Initially I had to see if it was possible to have a business that allows you the freedom to work from any location," said Vong. "We don't have the traditional office environment or corporate culture, having to show up at a set time. I wanted to offer the benefits of a traditional business along with the excitement of working in a startup. I guess this is what can be considered a "modern" working environment where our office water cooler is done on our social Slack channel."

In 2012 Vong took all of the things he'd learned and launched the business as a one-person consulting firm to create a proof of concept. "I had a very specific plan to make sure that I could do it by myself for one year so that I could learn it all and be responsible for everything," he said. "I couldn't blame anyone. When it came from back-office all the way to business development and project delivery, it was on me. I wanted to understand every aspect of my business that I would be asking someone else to do one day. After a short time, things began to grow. By being honest and working with our clients as partners, you tend to find those who believe in a shared vision of success. We still do not take on just any project that comes through the door. It's important that both sides value our time and honor our word when it comes to deliverables. This helped us out tremendously. We've never looked back. I brought in three other key folks who I consider co-founders of the company and we're officially at 15 people, which is not bad for a very short time frame."

The first issue to address was how to finance a business of this nature. As most entrepreneurs know, it typically comes down to one of two choices: either self-financing or using borrowed money. "We started off with the profits from my consulting business and rolled that into the company," said Vong. "When I look at the amount of consulting hours that we provide and the workload of the people, there's a very specific number that I target, meaning I don't want anyone on the team overworked for long durations. There are spikes and valleys in the workload but when it's consistent, we can project the need to hire more people."

EMPLOYEES ARE #1

Vong believes that if you care about how hard and how well people work from the get-go, you will set the stage for a truly successful company because the employees will care back. "They don't feel like you're exploiting them," he said. "It's always easy to find the very key people right away. But as you grow, you need more people and it becomes more of a second and third referral when you go to hire on the open market. You don't know the personality of the people you bring in right away. Our specific business is all about the people and the challenge is, how do I scale and keep the same level of delivery and quality to a client with the type of people we have? Also, we're now growing and, whereas all the senior folks used to do everything, now you don't have the same experience looking at a similar set of client challenges with each project. How do we assure a client that they're still getting what makes us very successful, which is the experienced team, versus junior people handling the problem? That's the challenge in growth for us, finding the right mix of talent, attitudes and shared ideals."

Currently, Vong is seeking new ways to enhance his business and maximize the value to his employees. "That is the overarching goal to determine success," he said. "We are very focused on a balance in terms of compensation, the ability to learn and grow professionally, and not having to sacrifice personal time to do it. We think about how best to provide this value to each and every person; that, in turn, is what helps to grow the company."

LOOK FOR WINNERS

Vong says the biggest growth area in his leadership skills has been in learning how to delegate day-to-day operational duties. "Entrepreneurs tend to do everything because they feel like they're the only one who can do it properly," he said. "There are things you might not be familiar with, from the bookkeeping to finances to HR rules and regulations, all the way to contract law. Those might not be your core skill sets but you are responsible for all of it. It's still overwhelming the number of things that I'm expected to know that I don't know and they're not why I started the business. However, I'm smart enough to just say I need an expert's opinion and go find that expert. How can one person keep up with everything that's going on?"

Another fact that Vong had to accept was that, when you run your own company, no matter what happens, every single person's issue becomes your issue. "If a client's unhappy, you have to understand or know the context of it," said Vong. "So that's the challenge, right? I have folks who are senior who I can delegate these things to but the challenge is to create a balance for yourself; that has been the most difficult challenge. Sometimes I wish I had more than 24 hours in the day but you really need to balance the work and personal life. You can't be unbalanced because then everything else goes unbalanced too."

NO BOUNDARIES

Digital Pi has grown its support team to the extent that they can handle most time zones in the United States, Europe and Asia. "The reason it works is that everyone on our team is a responsible adult and takes responsibility for their time," said Vong. "There is a huge trust factor and no one manages or watches the clock. There is complete trust that they will execute and plan their days accordingly. If you have folks who require a more "hands-on" management style or have an attitude that they must be told exactly what to do, they won't work well with our culture. For the level and type of work we do, location is definitely not a factor because we're able to cover more time zones and more scenarios with the tools we have in place. I won't hold our company to a U.S.-based four time zone concept because that's not how our clients work."

Vong was also alert to the financial benefits of not owning infrastructure because it allows the cost of consulting to remain lower and profits to soar higher without the fixed costs. "If you look at companies that have a physical location, more and more of them are allowing people to telecommute because they realize the benefits," said Vong. "People who telecommute or work remotely tend to work longer and harder because there is no water cooler time. Most are just a different breed of folks who have been self-managed their whole lives. Most people who work remotely do a lot more and, by comparison, perform much better."

PRIMARY CHALLENGES

As CEO of the company, Vong is constantly identifying and defending against factors that can change the business both externally and internally. "Externally, meaning threats to the business, competitors, climatology, environment and spending," he explained. "All of those changes have a very dramatic and very quick effect on the business. Then, there are some of the internal things like, how do you grow and maintain good employees? Because we are a consulting business, the value in everything we do is through the people who work on the project. So how do you keep a consistent level in every aspect of it? Their growth and happiness are all factors for us."

The hiring process can also be a difficult one, although Vong seems to have weeded out the chaff and found the top-notch folks in this business arena. "One hundred percent of our team came through referrals," said Vong. "They had a very solid background and were looking for an opportunity like this. What we need and the kind of thinking that we have is not easy to find. There are many smart people but the type of focus and skill sets and the attitude we are looking for are rare. I find those folks and try desperately to hire them. That's our competitive advantage but, as the talent pool drains, I think we definitely need a lot more folks in our industry."

GROWING CLIENTELE

Since the foundation of his business acumen was built in Silicon Valley, Vong still tends to attract a greater share of technology clients for his company. There's a healthy mixture of healthcare and retail clients that are beginning to emerge, but core technology companies are still their specialty. "The challenge with them is that they have a presence that tends to be global," said Vong. "For a small agency like ours, the question is how do we service across the globe and in all time zones? The challenge has always been to figure out ways to stagger time zones and that showcases the whole concept of remote employees. They tend to have more flexibility in terms of time to support clients, which also works with their schedules. We have a mixture of early birds and night owls and this has been a great experience for them."

Ultimately, Vong's clients know their business best because they compete in their industry every day. But what they may not see are similar issues that other companies deal with that might present a resolution they never thought about. "I think the benefit of what we do is to provide an outside expert opinion," said Vong. "Many times our clients will have a very specific need. We have the benefit of seeing what works and can make it work better. Through our experiences we learn how other companies solved similar problems. These companies are very smart; they just need a breath of perspective so they can make the right decision that fits their business."

This is where the collaborative nature of the work shines brightest. For example, Digital Pi may enter the retail industry with a client. They aren't experts in that industry but they are experts in the process. "The approach we take is the same across all industries," said Vong. "There are various methodologies for getting to a resolution, which are very similar no matter what industry. The industry perspective from our clients helps us tailor some of those processes. You normally go through a discovery process that has very specific and significant business questions and that's going to be the same for any industry. We help identify those factors that are generic and incumbent to all. Our process doesn't change because it's a new industry. We really partner with our client more and more about their specific business. We will learn the industry and the various nuances about how the company works and that's why the consulting is successful. We tune into those things and adjust our models to work for them."

PAY IT FORWARD

The mentoring that Vong received along the way has been a key component of the success he's now enjoying as the boss. The advice, the time and the vetting of issues have all been very insightful. "In turn, I do the same with the folks who are looking for that help and I can see that there is a desire to succeed," said Vong. "My time is extremely valuable but there is definitely a payback that is important. Go and help the next folks who are going through the same scenarios. I look at everybody I've mentored as someone I could potentially work for at some point. If you look in that direction and find the right folks you want to mentor, the mentoring doesn't stop. I have some very established folks in my network whom I reach out to about things that I just can't answer; things that they would know because they have gone through it. I still reach out for advice and help and, in turn, it pays right back through the folks I help groom within the company."

MAKE OR BREAK

There's a burning desire as an entrepreneur to do something great and Vong says you owe it to yourself to pursue it, no matter what the outcome is. "The process of getting there should never be about the outcome," he said. "It should be because you really have a burning desire to do this, to run your own life. When my first son was born, I remember thinking that I will one day tell him to do what he is passionate about and pursue his dreams. The clarity of that thought was that I can't tell him to do what I myself would not do."

VALUE CREATION

Entrepreneurs are addicted to creating entities that showcase the potential to create wealth. Although the payoff is important, that's never been Vong's ultimate motivation. "We look for like-minded people who are not asking for a 30-year role," he said. "This is not the environment for folks who think like that. My promise to everyone is that, within five years, we are going to create value in a company. That plan has an exit and an outcome and it could do something great or it could fail. That's a very risky thing but if they're willing to take the risk, I assure them that they will be rewarded. I lay out all the risks just to see what their reaction is because the ones who stay actually have the desire and are the ones we want. The company doesn't fit with the traditional mentality of folks who are only looking for a place with tenure and stability. We don't have anything like that here. This is a company that is going to make it or break it. Many things are under our control and we're looking for very specific people who feel the same way. It really is the most rewarding and the scariest high all at the same time. You just can't get it doing anything else."

"Kudos to the people who believed."

GREG JAMISON

FOUNDER / PRESIDENT

JAMISON ENTERTAINMENT GROUP

As a Sports Anchor, I usually dealt with players and coaches but I've always been fascinated by the behind-the-scenes activity in American professional sports. I was one of the Bay Area media "insiders" with the Sharks organization and knew that a lot was brewing in their front office, led by President and COO Greg Jamison. Greg was brought in by owner George Gund to take the helm and be responsible for the "little things"—if you call launching a franchise and keeping newbie hockey fans and sponsors happy "little" things. No worries. All in a day's work for an experienced pro like Greg Jamison.

PRO SPORTS BACKGROUND

Ten years prior to becoming the President and Chief Operating Officer of the National Hockey League's San Jose Sharks, Greg Jamison was already an accomplished team executive in the National Basketball Association. His first foray into professional sports was with the Dallas Mavericks in 1980 where he gained valuable knowledge about organizational methods. From there he went to the Indiana Pacers, where he learned the business side from the legendary Donnie Walsh. "Donnie was the president. He had been in basketball for a long time and I watched him build that team," said Jamison. "We did not make the playoffs in the early years but I was watching the team being built piece by piece. As he was building the team side, I was building the business side, so when the two became successful they could work well together."

Jamison also had a first-hand view of NBA Commissioner David Stern as he frantically worked to rebuild the NBA's less-than-stellar image that had the league hooked up to the life support system of late night tape delays and declining sponsorships. "Stern spent a lot of time marketing and I watched how he helped build the league into a global entity, partly because of the Olympics and partly because of the number of TV broadcasts," said Jamison. "Now there are well over 150 countries that can tune in to the NBA. It's those types of people who I learned a lot from. I took a lot from my Dallas experience and owner Don Carter then went to Indiana and took a lot from Herb and Mel Simon and Donnie Walsh. So when I came to San Jose I felt comfortable. Why wouldn't I want to do it when the opportunity availed itself? I had watched teams and organizations being built and that was our goal—to build a great sport and entertainment organization in San Jose."

WHERE'S SAN JOSE?

The first problem was that San Jose was a nontraditional hockey market. Ask a thousand people around the league and most would've had no clue how to find San Jose and Silicon Valley on a map. So when Jamison came to San Jose after being in the NBA for thirteen years it was a change, but the good thing was that the fundamentals stayed the same. "When I first came out here I thought this could be a battle," said Jamison. "But the business of sport is the business of sport, so I decided to do the normal business things. It's amazing the city took to it, the market took to it and it continued to grow. For a while we weren't very good on the ice, but then some things came together and we were able to take off. So I must admit that, while the market was learning hockey, I was also learning hockey and it became a sport that I developed incredible passion for."

COHESIVE STAFF

George Gund was the principal owner of the Sharks franchise and his first task was to develop a staff that worked as efficiently in the front office as a winning team would on the ice. "George hired strong building people, people who were strong in marketing and operations and others who really liked what they were doing and appreciated and understood the idea of what high end professional sport is all about," said Jamison. "Having the entire organization on the same page helped. At the end of the day you put your passion in and everybody is on the same page, going the same way to try to make this successful. It's amazing when a group of people is committed to growing something and working together. You can accomplish a lot of successful goals and that's what happened with the Sharks."

ADVERTISING CHALLENGES

When it came to selling advertising, there were some growing pains for the high tech world and San Jose businesses to work through. However, some of the early advertisers were people who had been transplanted from the East Coast who were used to seeing red jerseys and blue shirts skating on the ice. "The interesting thing about this phenomenon was folks from the sponsor world understanding that it could be carried at the local level," said Jamison. "A lot of people who, if you had told them a few years early, you're going to become a hockey fan, they would look at you like you had three heads. Eventually grownups began skating with their kids. Five-year old kids would say I want to grow up and play for the Sharks and the same enthusiasm carried over to the sponsors."

There needed to be an adaptation and an understanding of how to become a good sponsor of the Sharks. Everyone involved needed to learn how to make it a win-win-win-win for the sponsors, the company, the team and the arena. "There were some really creative ideas and eventually the whole league began to takes cues on how to do sponsorship," said Jamison. "We had some programs that were adapted by other markets but you can't do that without sponsorship. As we went along, more and more good sponsors came into the fold and the high tech world continued to grow in its role."

SERVE THE COMMUNITY

One of the reasons the Sharks took hold in the community was because of the innovative educational development programs that they filtered throughout the Bay Area. "The sports team in the market needs to give back to the market as much as possible," says Jamison. "So there were many community development and community relations programs that were formed. Street hockey, broom hockey and other programs went out as part of the education component. Kids went out on the playground and we developed programs that went on for years and years. I think the educational component was good and the arena component was really good. That was important because in the early years they wouldn't have known a blue line from a red line, what is offside, what is icing, what is all this stuff?"

One of the ideas that Jamison is most proud of is the reading program that the Sharks developed for local schools. "We worked with 21,000 students every year and encouraged kids to read," he said. "More teachers and more schools used that program each year and I like the fact that we became part of the fabric of the educational world."

From Day One, Jamison and the Sharks wanted fans to enjoy a good time in the arena, at the time, the most modern building in professional sports. "There were a lot of on-ice activities, a lot of things going on in the stands with the mascot, and all of those things that helped create a good fan experience," he remembered. "All those things that make you say I would come back to this place again. I may not know the game very well, but I'll learn. I would like to come back here because it's fun, it's easy and downtown is safe. All of those components were looked at and discussed and it came together really well."

SAN JOSE ARENA

The Sharks managed and ran the arena but it was bought, paid for and belonged to the City of San Jose. "The city is our partner and you never want to lose sight of that," said Jamison. "The city can help you and you can help the city. Every time the Sharks play you're bringing more than 17,000 people downtown. They're going to eat some place, they're going to stay somewhere. And that doesn't count the concerts, the circuses, the other family shows, the rodeos and all of the things that go with that. Consider the events that come here: the NCAA Men's and Women's basketball tournaments, ice skating and gymnastics, and many others; huge events that you never could have in your city if you didn't have the downtown arena. When you host 100 to 200 events per year that's bringing a lot of people downtown. So, kudos to all the people who believed in it and who stuck to it. I think it has been a really solid thing for the city of San Jose and Santa Clara County. Obviously Mayor Tom McEnery was a big component in getting that done and there's no question that San Jose voters did the right thing, yet I'm always reminded that the vote for the arena was only 51-49. But, today I'm not sure if anybody will say they voted against it."

FILL THE SEATS

The Sharks were an NHL expansion team, which meant they had to build primarily through the draft. Of course, if you need to do it that way, success will take a little bit longer. Bad teams don't normally draw fans but up the road in Oakland, the NBA team was bucking the odds year after disappointing year. "The Warriors, even when they weren't having great success on the floor, were having pretty good success in the seats and they built a really good fan base," said Jamison. "We tried to do the same things. Even if you're not winning you've still got to play the games and you still want people to be there, and you still want sponsors to be a part of it. It does make it a little bit easier when you win, let's be candid; everybody would agree to that. But there's still a lot of great marketing that goes on and some great merchandise ideas even when the team is not having good success. Overall, that's what happened. Many people in the beginning weren't sure if it was going to be successful in San Jose but that eventually subsided and the various city components learned to work together to make it a very good situation. Sometimes your team does not have success but you still can do things to have people come down and have a great fan experience."

GENERATE FUN

It's always fun to work on something that you enjoy doing. For Jamison, sports is still his toy chest. "When I went into professional sports in 1980 I never watched the clock and I always enjoyed what I did," he said. "I love sports, I love business and I love combining the two to help a team grow. I'm not talking about just the team on the field, ice or floor, but also the team in the front office. I liked putting something together, so being a part of NBA basketball or NHL hockey was always fun, exciting and challenging."

Like everything else, there's been a sea change in the sports marketing world from the time when Jamison began his career. The moneymaking part of it is where the biggest changes have occurred. "You've got to make sure that you can handle different types of pricing, that you can make enough revenue to offset the expenses," he said. "Many good marketing people get overshadowed by a team's dismal performance. That's always a little bit scary, but that's when you've got to be really good at what you're doing. You always hope that, when they look at the entertainment menu for Friday night, people will select you and not go to a movie or out to eat or miniature golfing. You want them to come and watch your product and that's something that every sports team works at. They want people to come and be a part of it."

NEXT VENTURE

Now that he's away from the NHL spotlight, Jamison and his son are working together in minor league hockey arenas. They own a team in Salt Lake City and another in Vancouver where his son is the team president. "I have enjoyed working with my son on this project and part of it is the same type of thing: A) recruiting players for your team B) going after sponsorships C) selling tickets and D) trying to be a part of the community," said Jamison. "It doesn't matter what level you're at, you're still doing the same kinds of things and that's why you have to adjust to the community you're working in. We certainly don't charge the same prices in Junior A that you might do in the NBA or NHL but you're still selling sponsorships and trying to get people involved. You want to be part of the community and you want the community to be proud of you. It doesn't matter if you're in the NHL, NBA, Major League Baseball or the NFL; you still want the community to be proud of you and for them to have an affinity for you. We do that at all levels. The things you learn are applicable in almost any job that we're engaged in."

COST MANAGEMENT

Jamison grew up as a big fan of the California Angels and he remembers attending games in the late 1970s, when ticket prices were less than today's bag of peanuts. "I used to spend $2 to sit in the upper deck and I had a great time," he remembered. "I wouldn't change it for the world. It was great fun just being a part of it. It's something that I think every league, every commissioner, every team owner and team has to deal with, the whole idea of trying to cover your costs while making it an affordable product. It's a real dynamic tension. You're doing a lot to make it successful but in the same vein it's expensive. You've got everything from payroll to general expenses, from travel to all the expenses that go into putting on a product like that. You've got to have enough revenue to offset that. So, where do you get the revenue? You get it from tickets, from sponsorships, from broadcasts and from various components. It's a real tough spot and that's why how creative you can be is critical. It isn't always how much money you spend on payroll, it's what kind of team you put together that sets you apart. I think those are the things that have to be taken into consideration when you do this. This is one of the problems that every team has to face—to make it affordable, yet be able to generate enough revenue to offset the expense."

FREE ADVICE

Jamison says he's still up to speed on technology, in the sense that he uses social media to develop and maintain his business. However, face-to-face is still his preferred method of communication. "LinkedIn is amazing," Jamison says. "It's just one of the vehicles that allow you to stay connected with people. But, I would encourage a young entrepreneur not to just rely on social media but to actually go and have a conversation with somebody. Feel free to drop a note and maintain your relationships. The relationships make business in most industries go 'round. Successful entrepreneurs are known for their product but they've really built up and maintained connections. I still have relationships from 1980 all the way through different teams, different cities and markets. I'm a firm believer that if you help others become successful you have a chance of being successful as well. That's the way to approach it and I think those really good and successful people all do it that way."

"Man, there's nothing that beats that!"

RON GONZALES
PRESIDENT / CEO
HISPANIC FOUNDATION

It wasn't all that long ago when people around the world still did not know the way to San Jose. However, by the late 1990s, Silicon Valley fortunes had blossomed, thanks in large part to redevelopment funds that helped entrepreneurs launch their companies. Ron Gonzales was mayor from 1999-2007 and helped oversee much of the growth that continues to define the entrepreneurial spirit of the Valley. Now, a decade after leaving public office, Ron's focus is on helping those sharing his Hispanic heritage to earn a piece of that explosive success.

MAYOR RON

When he was elected Mayor of San Jose in 1998, Ron Gonzales was not only the first San Jose mayor of Latino descent since statehood, he was also the first mayor to boast of a high tech background. "I spent many years at Hewlett Packard in various roles," said Gonzales. "Certainly, having knowledge of the industry helped me lead the city. In many areas our city services were not nimble enough to respond to an ever-changing industry. Getting our workforce and our leadership to recognize that just because a company's headquarters is in San Jose now, it doesn't mean they are going to stay there forever. We had to be in constant communication with our leading employers, understanding what their needs were, what we could anticipate and change in terms of city policies and practices, and put the city in a position where these entrepreneurs saw us as a resource rather than a deficit. There is always a difficult balance between the company needs versus the city's needs."

HELPING STARTUPS

One of the things the city did for startups was lower the price for a business license. But the best thing that San Jose had going for it at that time was the Redevelopment Agency. The agency, implementing California redevelopment law, provided incredible financial resources for the city to utilize on startups. "I think we used the funds more effectively than many other cities in terms of creating things like our Bio-Tech Incubator Project that helped new start-up companies get the first couple of years under their belt at a very low cost," said Gonzales. "We even accommodated the construction of wet and dry labs for the bio-tech industry and that drew many companies to south San Jose where we needed to create jobs because the land wasn't being developed as quickly as other parts of the county."

Gonzales stewarded those redevelopment funds effectively to not only help employers place jobs in San Jose, but also to build affordable housing; eleven thousand affordable homes were constructed in an eight year period of time. "The city staff told me that was more affordable housing built by any California city, including Los Angeles, over that same eight year period," said Gonzales. "Why was that important? Well, you can't recruit jobs if you don't have a place for workers to live. When most people think of affordable housing, they think about the old HUD programs but affordable housing is actually for families that earn 80% of the median income for the region. So it's more for low-middle income workers and many start-ups could only offer those kinds of salaries."

The city also studied transportation options to get workers from where they lived to where they worked and back home in time for dinner. "That was my motto and how we evaluated our transportation system," said Gonzales. "All these things make up the quality of life that helps draw and retain employers in your community."

San Jose was seen as a model city throughout America but Gonzales also credits the surrounding Silicon Valley cities for their efforts. "This region is quite frankly lusted after by many mayors, not only in the United States but also throughout the world," he said. "You see governors and mayors coming through Silicon Valley, trying to recruit industry from here to create jobs in their communities. Now, of course, many of these industries have in fact placed many of their jobs in other countries or other parts of the United States. But the brain trust stays right here in Silicon Valley—the research and development labs, the places where new ideas and new products are created."

HISPANIC FOUNDATION

At the end of 2006, Gonzales and his wife Guisselle opened a marketing consulting company but they have stopped taking on new clients, primarily because of his top level job at the Hispanic Foundation of Silicon Valley. "As its President and CEO it's a full time job in itself," says the former mayor. "I've got a 'gigantic' staff of four people and actually two of them are part-time. But I prefer a small, efficient team where we are getting as much money to meet the community needs as we possibly can."

In his current role, Gonzales seeks out opportunities to meet Latino entrepreneurs who need guidance but he's also looking for those who can teach up-and-coming business owners. "We're always looking for Latino business leaders and people who are doing well in business," he says. "I'm proud to say that we do have more than we had a decade ago. Not as many as we would like to see, but I do come across some business people who I used to interact with as the Mayor of San Jose."

IMPROVE PERFORMANCE

Unfortunately for the Latino community, many of the problems that hinder their financial success are due to a high dropout rate. The Hispanic Foundation is tasked to help improve the performance of Latino students from middle school all the way to college. "We are studying how we can do a better job of growing engineers and computer scientists from our own neighborhoods rather than having to import them from other parts of the world," says Gonzales. "Nothing wrong with that either, but there's a work force here that, if properly trained and educated, can do those jobs without the cost of relocating people from other parts of the world. When I was mayor I met regularly with all 19 school district superintendents. We listened to them and created city-funded programs that met their needs."

114

HAND OVER THE KEYS

The biggest need in San Jose at that time was retaining teachers in a metro area that's very expensive to live in. The mayor's office used redevelopment dollars to help 530 teachers buy their first home in the city of San Jose. "That meant they got to stay here and teach here and live here and be tax paying residents in the city where they taught," said Gonzales. "Of all the things I've ever done as mayor, probably the most delightful experience I've ever had was handing over the keys to the first house of a young couple. Man, there is nothing that beats that. That was a lot of fun."

It's a rare week when someone doesn't credit Gonzales for his efforts to create roots for teachers and their families. "Every time we got to one hundred, then two hundred, then the three hundredth house that we helped purchase, we'd have a little press conference," he said. "I remember when we got to four hundred we went out to a townhouse over in the northeast section of San Jose. The wife was a kindergarten teacher and the husband was a high school math and science teacher. The husband came up and thanked me profusely for the program. I found out that he had previously worked in high–tech. I said, wait a second, how can you afford to move from a high-tech job to a teacher salary? He says, *'Mayor, what you don't understand is that teaching was always my dream. I was doing the high-tech job so that we could save up enough money to buy a house. When your program came along it allowed me to pursue my dream to be a teacher.'* Wow, two teachers staying in San Jose. Bingo! Man leaves high-tech to become a math/science teacher. Bingo! They're both living in San Jose and paying taxes. Bingo! So, it was like a super bingo day and that kind of experience is not easy to forget. I remember it like it was yesterday."

A NEW ERA

There are more people these days, Latino and non-Latino, who can't picture themselves working for someone else long term. They recognize that, for the amount of labor they'd put into a job for 20 years, the returns will not be as good as if it were their own business. "I hear more and more Millennials asking, what is the point of me doing all this when I'm not going to reap the benefits?" said Gonzales. "I think that's a mindset that you find a lot more extensively with younger people, even in the Latino community. What's the point of working for someone else when the assets of that work belong to them and not to me?"

If you're attracted to a life of entrepreneurship, there is probably no better region in the world to be situated in than Silicon Valley. This is a region that rewards risk takers, people who dare to try something different and who follow the path less traveled. "It's often been said that people in Silicon Valley are not considered successful unless they've failed a couple of times, because that means you're out there pushing the envelope of innovation and entrepreneurship," says Gonzales. "So you couldn't be in a better place to pursue that dream; you should certainly pursue it and not give up on it."

You've heard this from athletes, actors and professionals in every occupation who excel through adversity: they never listened to the people who told them it was impossible. "The value of being in Silicon Valley is that you're not going to find many people who tell you it's not possible," said Gonzales. "They are going to tell you why it should be possible and that's a big difference. So whether they are Latino or not I encourage their desire and make sure they fully understand that pursuing it is not going to be easy. It's running your business and getting your product to the marketplace. There is nothing more rewarding than to have that first customer. The second most rewarding thing is having your second customer."

One of the challenges these days is that products and services change rapidly so the high-tech industry has a hard time telling college students what skills they're going to need in five years. "These days they'll tell you they are always looking for those who are entrepreneurial, who view themselves as both a team player and an individual contributor," says Gonzales. "Back in the day, when we were first becoming employed, most companies were looking for team players only, not individual contributors. Well, now the companies that succeed are the ones that have both and accommodate each style."

LEADERSHIP ACADEMY

Gonzales and his staff keep their radar focused for ambitious individuals who carry the entrepreneurial spirit. "We have a program that we call the Latino Board Leadership Academy where we train young Latinos who want to serve on the Board of Directors for non-profit organizations," he said. "Last May we graduated our fifth academy and we've trained nearly 200 people. Seventy-five percent of them have been appointed to a Bay Area non-profit Board of Directors. What you have to understand with the Hispanic community is that we're very diverse. Some of us are the children of first generation immigrants, others are second or third generation. The reality is, when you get into fourth, fifth and sixth generations you become more and more assimilated, so your connection with the community may not be as strong."

Many young people have grown up in a family business where everybody pulls the load. Ron's wife worked in her family's travel industry business but her generation didn't see that as a career. "That's probably true for a lot of small businesses where the next generation has no interest," says Gonzales. "I think that will diversify itself over a period of time. They know it's a lot of work and even though you're working for yourself, what do you have at the end of all of this?"

Gonzales says he always gives the benefit of the doubt to someone who looks interesting and does his best to introduce him to business owners who can help. "Nine times out of the ten they say yes, they want to talk, they want to learn about us and in doing that I can learn about their journey," says Gonzales. "It's interesting, I have found high level executives in Fortune 100 companies right here in Silicon Valley who our young people don't know about. We're going to do something about that as we become more mature as a foundation, hopefully under my leadership."

CALLING ALL MENTORS

Gonzales is proud of his heritage and knows that Latino kids can, indeed, reach the top of any field. His key is finding the right mentors who are willing to lift them to the top. "I think it's helpful and it leads to greater success if we have a mentor who's been through it before," says Gonzales. "That person doesn't necessarily have to be Latino. It's helpful when they are but it has to be someone who understands that this particular Latino's path to entrepreneurship may not be the same one that he or she took."

Gonzales says the biggest obstacle that Latino entrepreneurs need to overcome is access to capital. Like many aspects of business, the winning formula centers on relationships. "We don't necessarily go to the same universities that some of the venture capitalists go to," says Gonzales. "I've heard companies that say, unless you've got a degree from Stanford we're not going to take time to interview you. They won't say that publicly but I know they have said it privately to individuals. If you're a venture capitalist and you've invested in a Latino whose first business was a success, that should tell you something, because that person had to overcome things that many of your other recipients did not have to. Our Hispanic culture is known for its hard work, determination and, in some respects, a positive stubbornness; we don't give up easily. I think those are the characteristics of Latinos and other minority groups."

SET FOR THE FUTURE

The Hispanic Foundation has two new initiatives that are soon to be launched. The first is a robust scholarship program for Latinos students who are majoring in what are called STEM degrees: Science, Technology, Engineering and Math. "We hope to be in a position financially where we can help at least one hundred students per year for an initial five-year period," said Gonzales. "So, in five years we would have helped 500 students complete their bachelor's degree in either computer science, engineering, or something related to the field."

The second initiative is called the Family College Success Center. "In the Latino community, going to college, particular for the first generation student, is a family decision," says Gonzales. "It's not just the child saying, *'I'm going to go to UC Berkeley or I'm going to go to MIT'*. It's a family decision, particularly when that child is a female. So, we want to make sure that we have done our job to educate those parents with all the information they need to make that decision. We hope to open this center where an entire family can take advantage of our programs. We'll recruit from local universities and colleges to help prepare families and their children to graduate from college."

EMBRACE MENTORING

Looking back on a stellar career as a high tech executive and the mayor of a leading American city, Gonzales points to mentorship as a key that he feels is mandatory in order to rise to the level of success. "I am 100 percent, even 1000 percent behind the concept of mentorship," he said. "If I were to give one key bit of advice to a young person wanting to be successful in life, whether it's owning their own business or excelling in someone else's business, it's to have that mentor. Have that person who will tell you what you need to know, not necessarily what you want to know. I had those people working for me as mayor. Sometimes I think that we don't easily acknowledge the value of experience. Young people view our experience as irrelevant because today's world is so different than last century's world. But it is relevant because you're still identifying goals and dreams and visions and trying to achieve them, and we know how to do that. If you have the right mentors, they'll be very helpful, not only in terms of your career, but also in terms of personal life and other factors that affect your career. Young people tend to divide the two but as experienced people, we know that the personal stuff is part of the business stuff. It's not inseparable anymore."

"Dang, either this doesn't work or I suck at it."

TERE KAMPE

INTERNATIONAL MARKETING DIRECTOR

WORLD VENTURES

I've discovered that Tere Kampe is a "Get 'er done" kind of guy. He's no nonsense when it comes to taking on a task and completing it. Maybe that's why he's vaulted himself into the upper echelon of his network marketing business. Tere is teaching his Northern California lineage how to build a team and reminding us that the blood, sweat and tears that we invest over the next few years will create residual income for the rest of our lives. He's a real winner with a humbling story about the days when he didn't quite feel like championship material.

FRUSTRATIONS

Amway specializes in personal care and nutritional products and, since 1959, has built an independent business owner force of more than three million people all around the world. Among those reps are Tere Kampe's parents, who have devoted more than four decades of their lives to their business in one of the world's oldest network marketing companies. "When I was ten years old I was around network marketing and I got a unique perspective," said Kampe. "Along the way I got to see that business in its infancy. My dad was horribly introverted but he held a meeting every Wednesday night. Every Wednesday night he'd show me the plan or he'd show my dog the plan but he never actually invited anybody because he was afraid to do that."

Kampe's parents reached the Director level in the Amway business hierarchy but remained stuck at that level for 38 years. For Tere, that was as frustrating as could be. "As I watched this happen, I saw them be the support people for all the successful people," he said. "They were never the successful people. The other people were the successful people. My parents were the ones who did all the work to help the successful people be successful. So, I had these self-limiting beliefs, this bar of success for my family, that we only get to be this successful but no more. Because that's who I am and that's the family I was born into. That's what I heard over and over. I heard a lot about dreams, I heard a lot about goals, I heard a lot about success but I never saw it at home. So, one of the things I eventually had to recognize was that I had that stuff inside me. All of you have the same thing going on. You have a bar of success that you've put on yourself and most of you don't even know it."

MAYBE IT'LL WORK THIS TIME

For twenty years Kampe's parents plugged away on their Amway business and he wanted nothing to do with it. He saw what his parents had to do and he didn't want to be similarly trapped. But, "After the 20th year they got hooked up with another guy who built things much differently," said Kampe. "I saw that and all of a sudden I was interested because of the results he was getting. So I jumped into that, saying, 'I'm going to kill it'. I thought everybody I knew was going to join me. So I jumped into Amway and for six years I did it. Six years, every single night, tape after tape after tape, meeting after meeting after meeting after meeting. After six years, two thousand nights doing that deal, I had fifty people on my team. Fifty. It was awesome!"

Anyone who knows Kampe's personality knows that when he makes a commitment to something, the work is going to get done. He was all in, at the expense of his family life. "You know birthdays, holidays, all that stuff can wait until we get it done," he said. "Anybody know what personality type that is? Red. Yes, sir. That was me and I outworked everybody but I could not reproduce me to save my life. I don't know why because I just figured somebody else out there would want to work as hard as I was working and get the results I was getting but that didn't really happen."

DO I SUCK AT THIS?

There are at least two things that Kampe says you need to keep in mind when you undertake a network marketing business: 1) You've got to believe in you and 2) You've got to believe in your business. But somewhere along the way one of those two things usually trips people up. "After six years I started asking the question," recalled Kampe. "Dang, either this doesn't work or I suck at it, one of the two. At that point my belief cracked so I stopped. I quit. Even though I was technically in, I had quit. I was never going to do this again. But keep in mind what I said before; I had watched 2,000 days of tape after tape after tape, so I was growing Me even though it didn't really look like that based on my results. You get the picture?"

Once he decided he was completely done with the Amway business, Kampe told himself he would never do network marketing again. At this point, he was tired and cynical about the whole industry. "I was done trying to help people because I'd given a lot of time and effort to a lot of people and they didn't do the things they said they were going to do," said Kampe. "You know people like that? They deceive you because they say they're going to do this but then they don't and we don't understand. So I decided I was just going to take care of me and my family and that's what I did. I began selling chemicals to semiconductor companies and after about seventeen years I was working only fifteen hours a week from my couch while making a pretty good income. My wife didn't work and life was really cool. I was an elder at my church so I gave them a lot of time."

FATEFUL CALL

But one day Kampe received a phone call from Doug Shiplett, a long-time friend and the pastor who married Tere and Mary in San Jose. The Shipletts had left the Bay Area and moved to Iowa but Doug had an urgent message for Kampe. "He called me, *'Dude, you got to check this out.'* Whenever somebody made that phone call, I knew what that meant," said Kampe. "So I'm like, yes Doug, yes, yes, yes, yes. He was really excited about it but I was going to go get him out of whatever it was he was trying to get me into."

Shiplett eventually sent a video featuring chiropractor David Pietsch, one of the highest ranking WorldVentures reps, but Kampe said he didn't understand the concept. "The next video he sends me is Scott Ross in a pair of shorts and sandals with a white screen behind him and I'm like, why is that guy wearing shorts and sandals? I don't get it," said Kampe. "The second time through it, I still didn't know it was travel. But I decided to do it anyway. My wife wanted nothing to do with this, I mean nothing. With Amway, we'd get done with work and then drive three hours to Bakersfield for a meeting and no one would be there. Not even the people who were in the business. So we'd drive three hours back and she's seven months pregnant. Then we'd get up at 6:00am to go back to work. That's where we both were with network marketing."

HEY, THIS MIGHT WORK!

But something inside told Kampe to keep an open mind to the WorldVentures idea. So he did what he knew best, taking the next month to pray through his decision. "Most everybody who sees WorldVentures asks, *'Can I do this?'* I was asking myself, 'Am I ready to do this again?' Because when I got started in San Jose it was just me; my sponsor was in Iowa and the nearest thing going on was six hours away in LA," said Kampe. I had to ask myself, 'Am I really going to do this and build everything that has to be built?' Whatever happened had to be me making it happen. But after about a month I said yes, I'm going to do this thing. Doug flew out from Iowa to put me in the system and I had enough sense to call some people over that night. My wife would not come downstairs to watch the video. I'm telling you, she wanted nothing to do with this." *(Bonus training: "If your spouse does not want to do this, do it anyway.*

For real. Guys, zip it up, be the man and go do it. Don't wait for your wife's approval. Do it anyway. She will thank you.")

Kampe worked hard and discovered early success through WorldVentures. He moved steadily up the ranks but, once he achieved Marketing Director status, he found himself at a mental crossroads. "When I jumped into this thing, Regional Marketing Director was the level that other people got to," said Kampe. "So I set my goal for Marketing Director. Why? Because that's where I believed I deserved to be. RMD was beyond my bar of success. Eighty-five percent of everything that happened the first year was because of me doing the work. We hit Director in about a year and in two years we hit Marketing Director. My wife had started to come along because, of course, she realized it was vacations and not soap and vitamins."

CREEPING DOUBT

Another six months went by as Kampe worked to reach the RMD level but he still couldn't shake the feeling that RMD was beyond what he deserved. In addition, some distracting issues were beginning to shred the fabric of his team. "I had a couple of Directors but both of them were out of the picture," says Kampe. "One was in another country for four months and the other one was totally disengaged. I had another guy who got suspended by the company for IRS stuff that happened years before; all kinds of junk was happening. I had leaders who were fighting each other and there was a bunch of infighting happening. Most of my upline didn't even know we were in the business. We're out in San Jose just doing our thing so I had no one to ask how to fix the problem."

We all have days when we wish we could just pull the covers over our heads, shut the world out, and go back to sleep. For Kampe, there is one day that fits that description to a T. "I woke up one morning and ten percent of my team had quit," he said. "Overnight, all gone. Plus, I've got all this stuff going with my leaders. I called Tom Goris who was an International Marketing Director and said, 'Dude, I quit. I'm done.' I didn't know how to fix this and all I knew was to start asking God for help. Here I am 2-1/2 years in, I had left my job eighteen months before so I've got no job to go to. I'm quitting because it's not working and now all of a sudden I'm hearing all those voices in my head: *Your family doesn't deserve this excess; This is beyond you; This is as successful as you get to be.* That's what I'd experienced in my family forever and ever. This is as successful as I get to be, no more. So all I knew was to quit because I didn't know how to reach the next level. All I knew was the voices in my head are telling me this is as far as you get to go."

BREAK THAT MINDSET

Kampe reminds us all that we will face the same type of psychological obstacle—as he puts it, new levels, new devils. "As soon as you're ready to get to that next level you're going to experience turbulence and conflict in your life," says Kampe. "Whether it's Senior Rep or Director, that next level is beyond the person you have grown to be so far. When you get to that point you'll start to feel the tension and things will start going on and you'll begin to make excuses and start to question yourself. All those things will happen because your past is talking to your present about your future until you change the picture of your future. You got in this for a reason so there is this picture of life that you would like to have but you've got to go through a barrier to get to the new You. You reach the point where it's you who has to change; you have to grow, develop new habits, respond to people differently and care about people differently."

Albert Einstein was famous for saying as long as you keep doing things the way you have, you're going to keep getting the same results. Kampe makes it clear that you have to grow to reach that next level of success. "For most people, you're not going past Marketing Director without growing You," he said. "So, back to that time when all I knew how to do was quit. Because I didn't have a job, I called them back later that day and said I'm getting back in because I need to eat. I'm like, 'OK, God. You said to do this. You said You wanted me here. I need some help because I don't know how to fix what's going on.' After all was said and done, I realized I needed to grow Me."

Kampe says the distractions that were happening turned out to be a leadership issue on his part. As he recognized that and took command of his own destiny, he resolved to deal with the issues instead of merely allowing them to fester. "I picked up the phone and started calling my leaders to deal with what was going on," he recalled. "I kept showing the plan, even though it was still only me. Through the holidays I just kept showing it and I'm like, man, I'm the only one doing this. Everybody else is enjoying the holidays but I only had X amount of money in the bank and every dollar I made bought me more time. When 10% of the team backed out that morning it took a lot of my time away. The Bay Area is one of the most expensive places in the world so if you're making $30,000, it's not going very far. So, I'm struggling but I keep doing the work. Along the way there was all this nonsense in my head but I finally had to stop looking at me through my past and start looking at me the way God created me to be, and who God created me to be."

WE MADE IT!

Kampe knew deep inside that he was created for more so he chose to believe God and what He was saying versus what his past was saying about him. "I kept showing the plan but it wasn't really going all that well," he said. "I realized I had to get some other lineage going. So I started building and put on a whole mess of miles and in February, six months from the day when I called to quit, we hit RMD. During the travel party I was doing, I was watching my back office and noticed some people had jumped in who had no business getting in, other than God was answering my prayer. We had 22 people jump in on the last day of February and when I hit RMD, immediately all the voices went away."

Kampe has now reached International Marketing Director, the highest level of the WorldVentures business. His late push at the end of 2015 was supported and cheered throughout his lengthy lineage. "I want to encourage you guys that you were created for greatness," said Kampe. "But you have to allow yourself to step into that greatness. You have to give yourself permission to walk there. You have to give yourself permission to be as successful as you want to be. You can look around at other people and you can look at circumstances. It's still within you to create whatever you want to happen. It's probably going to take time because you have to dilute all the stinking thinking with new information. It takes time. You've got to listen to CDs and get around people who outthink you so that you learn to think at a different level. With more positive activity, the faster you'll begin to dilute the junk."

IT CAN BE YOURS

Kampe has stuck with the program and reminds us all that, if you do the same thing with the same diligence, you will become who you were created to be and you'll get to impact lives along the way. "Lives you won't even know, people you may not even meet, you'll get to impact. But you've got to step into that responsibility and own it for your life first and then for everybody else," says Kampe. "It's like we were climbing a mountain and when we got to RMD we were peeking over the first cliff. I had this picture that we're climbing this mountain and I'm looking over and yelling back, 'Man, the view is good but we've got to keep climbing.' The view is pretty good at RMD but it's not a stopping point. I mean, think about having total freedom in your life to do whatever you choose to do. No one gets to tell you who to be, where to be, when to be or how to be. You get to decide."

Most of us have self-imposed walls and barriers that we erect that lead to failure, or worse, non-participation in life. Things can change and you can put yourself back in control. "You ask people, 'What do you want life to look like five years from now?' and most of them stumble over the answer. But if you ask them what they don't want life to look like, they can give you all kinds of answers because all these walls are up," says Kampe. "All these barriers block the way of freeing your mind up. You've got to get that stuff out of the way by growing You. I just want to encourage you guys; the journey is worth it but you have to decide to take ownership. I want to encourage you to go be who God created you to be."

"We were good to go!"

TAM O'CONNOR FRASER

CO-FOUNDER

TAM COMMUNICATIONS

Owning a video production company is a goal for many traditional media people but few of them actually do it. I have done a lot of television production work, but never at the volume of Tam O'Connor Fraser. He had a full blown million dollar production company and soared to the top with great syndicated programming. His team stood out as one of the top video agencies in Northern California but the tide turned on 9/11 when running a big operation suddenly became like saving the Titanic. But save it he did as you'll read about in Tam's lesson in hard knocks.

COAST GUARD

Tam O'Connor Fraser began his work in syndicated television back in 1994 with a program titled *Coast Guard*, a reality show about the U.S. Coast Guard that ran for three years in the United States and internationally. The show was cleared in 125 markets, which allowed O'Connor Fraser to develop strong roots in the syndicated TV market of that era. "We created that and ran it as a pilot," he says. "We were looking for a syndicator, somebody who could clear the markets. Clearing markets is a whole different ballgame; you've got to have somebody who really knows what they're doing."

Coast Guard had been passed over by almost everybody and the project was on its last legs when an old friend referred O'Connor Fraser to Dick Perin, a small New York distributor who enjoyed that type of show. "He sent the pilot to one of those old school New York syndicators and we went to NATPE that year and started clearing markets," said O'Connor Fraser. "There was a competing show but we ended up beating them out. Then we cleared with the CBS O-and-Os, which was huge because they had all the big markets. Once we cleared CBS, this thing just took off and we were good to go!"

Tam Communications financed and produced the entire project. At the time he had a full-time staff of fifty, with offices on the 7th floor of a downtown San Jose high rise. "We invested nearly a million dollars in production and post-production facilities, which provided us the opportunity to develop projects independently and led to a relationship with Discovery Networks," said O'Connor Fraser. "We bought our own camera so we were able to do all those projects which led us into the Discovery Networks."

THE SYNDICATION GAME

Prior to *Coast Guard*, Fraser produced four episodes of *Paramedics 10-97* a reality show that aired on KNTV in San Jose. That idea was sold to a fledgling cable health network. O'Connor Fraser's wife, Susan, then suggested the idea to develop the *Coast Guard* series. "Many of the deals we did with Discovery at that point were co-productions which meant that they would cover half the budget," said O'Connor Fraser. "This gave them domestic rights for five years while we retained international rights. Owning the product is always the challenge. For the most part, it's considered work-for-hire. There are many production companies out there that make a lot of money doing work-for-hire but they don't own the final product."

The old saying reminds us that timing is everything. O'Connor Fraser got in at the tail end of the syndication boom but since then the rules have changed. As conglomerates purchased more and more TV stations, syndication became a much tougher way to make a living. "Many syndicators went out of business," said O'Connor Fraser. "The big syndicators would come in there and say, *'Well, if you want our show you're going to have to take this other stuff that we have.'* That systematically cut everybody out of the picture. Syndication is not a viable place for the smaller people anymore. Some guys are still carving it out but it's really a hard road."

REALITY (TV) BITES

The cable business has also changed drastically. Tam Communications was providing a good amount of prime time material for Discovery Channel but the work fell off as the network began airing more half-hour weekly programs. "In 2013 we pitched an idea to National

133

Geographic called *Life on a Farm*, then went out and shot a teaser with a family in Southwestern Virginia," said O'Connor Fraser. "They were cattle farmers and really funny people. The executives were looking for a *Duck Dynasty*-type show on National Geographic, which seemed odd to me. Within five minutes of viewing the teaser they called us and cut a deal. The thing is, we had to partner up with a big production house out of LA. They said we love what you guys have done but we haven't worked with you before. We know you have experience but if we give you the order for the show we need to know that it's with somebody who can really handle it. That was OK because I don't have the infrastructure that I once had. I still had gear but nowhere near what you need to pull off a show like that. So we ended up partnering with a big company out in LA called Authentic Entertainment."

The show took on a life of its own but is now called *Family Beef*. "They took our characters and changed our approach," said O'Connor Fraser. "We planned to follow the family and shoot whatever happened but they chose to feed the lines to them so the reality TV became more scripted."

O'Connor Fraser says he got spoiled with *Coast Guard* because he didn't have to take network feedback on the content. As you might imagine, it's difficult to relinquish control after you've developed your own product for syndication. "Since they were all co-productions we also had control over the creative and the storytelling approach," said O'Connor Fraser. "Discovery would guide us during post-production and we would work together to finalize the end product. But now they've got two executive producers assigned to you and some are easier to work with than others. Our interest in developing cable reality shows fell off after *Family Beef*, mainly because we're not interested in producing scripted reality shows that depend on over the top characters creating conflict. It's just not that interesting anymore."

PROVIDE VALUE

Traditional video production companies are getting squeezed from both ends. They're in a price war with the wannabes and studios, and expensive equipment and producer teams have become luxuries. Paydays are not as lucrative and now there's direct competition with ad agencies, marketing consultants and online media companies.

The value today is not in how you make the video but in how you apply the video to your market. Social media, interactive video and mobile video are developed for a specific business purpose. Companies now specialize in Human Relations or Public Relations videos as internal and vertical knowledge surpasses general production knowledge.

The Santa Cruz Beach Boardwalk is a great example of this new video trend. The Boardwalk attracts more than three million visitors per year and has been O'Connor Fraser's bread and butter client since 1992, when he began producing their TV commercials. "They left us for about a year," he said. "The VP of Marketing wanted to break things up and try something new but they failed miserably. It just didn't resonate so they came back to us and we've had them ever since."

In 2007 O'Connor Fraser produced a 90-minute DVD celebrating the 100th anniversary of the Boardwalk that was popular enough to trigger a deal with KQED to air the show for the next year. In 2008 Boardwalk management paid for a "look live" half-hour TV special and since then they've aired the yearly summer specials on KTVU. "In 2013, Susan shook things up and pitched the idea of a docu-reality approach," said O'Connor Fraser. "We did *A Day in the Life* of the park, following a little boy on his rite of passage aboard the world famous *Giant Dipper*, and that really resonated with viewers. We put a casting call out for somebody who would like to propose on the Boardwalk, then followed this guy around with his fiancé until he made his proposal to her. We covered it all with cameras and it was a total surprise. That program was #2 in its time slot, which was crazy for a paid program but it really caught viewers' attention."

For a number of years the Beach Boardwalk spots consisted of only music, a jingle and a narrator. Continuing the modern twist, O'Connor Fraser decided to feature people who were experiencing the park. "This year we got a group of teens to sing to the camera with each person singing different parts," he said. "We really brought it to the next level. Look at the Great America spots and they probably spend five times what the Boardwalk spends with us but I think our spots just beat the crap out of theirs."

Based on that success, O'Connor Fraser plans to take the Boardwalk concept to other accounts to see how they might also create half-hour TV programs, structuring deals with local stations where the client buys the airtime or by trying to attract eyeballs with a bartered show.

MAKE THE CLIENT HAPPY

As a producer, O'Connor Fraser occasionally struggles with wannabe corporate types who find it irresistible to constantly give their feedback on a post-production project. "I always find it interesting when they want this and they want that, but they really don't know what they're talking about," says O'Connor Fraser. "You've got to balance the fine line of getting them what they want while also making the right decision. By and large we seem to get our way more times than not but there have been a few times when I've had to do my own cut and then the client's cut, knowing our cut is better. But at the end of the day we have to make it work because they're the ones putting up the money and we really have to adhere to that."

With some editors, the ego gets in the way and it can result in the loss of thousands, or millions, of dollars in business. "We know of an advertising agency that lost an account because of their ego," said O'Connor Fraser. "All the client wanted was an additional two or three seconds of their product in a commercial but the editor refused to do it. Needless to say, they ended up losing the multi-million dollar account."

UPS AND DOWNS

The traditional production company is constantly involved in a bidding process unless they're able to find a client or two that will sign a guaranteed contract. "You always feel like business can go away at any point," says O'Connor Fraser. "Somebody can take over a new job and say *'I've got a fresh company that I want to work with'*. We've seen that happen time and time again."

While the Boardwalk has been loyal to O'Connor Fraser, and vice versa, he typically sees a four to five year run with most clients. "You need to not let them become so much of your business," he said. "We always make sure that we're into different things and have X amount of tech clients and Y amount of non-tech. We were doing all of West Marine's national TV spots for years but they decided to cut back when they got hit by the recession. They really had a hard time but they're finally coming back around and we just signed to do their radio commercials for next year. They're also talking about getting back into TV again which is a good thing for us."

TIMING IS EVERYTHING

Tam Communications was formed as Tam Productions in 1979, when the barrier for entry was ridiculously high. They invested nearly $1,000,000 in a post-production facility and at one point had four Avid editing systems in the house. It was considerably more expensive to create that kind of a business model back then than it is today. "When I had the big operation and I was making lots of money, I projected where I was going to be today," reflects O'Connor Fraser. "I always thought it was going to be good. Hey, when you're on top like that you just go all out. I have this big organization, millions to make, I've got my 401k and everything is good. What could go wrong? What could possibly go wrong?"

What could go wrong was what did go wrong for all of us on September 11, 2001. "We moved from downtown San Jose on September 10th, into an office on the Borland Campus in Scott's Valley," recalls O'Connor Fraser. "It was a beautiful 40,000 square foot place. Then 9/11 hit and everything just started dropping. One of our big accounts had done a million dollars that year but shut down on us. Then the dominoes started falling one after another and it just kept on going. Within two years I was down to a staff of six. From that time on it became a struggle. I still had all these facilities with all the equipment. I had the skeletal remains of the infrastructure but I didn't have any more staff so I just plugged away. I kept my editor and we operated like that for three more years before moving into a new space."

BACK IN THE GROOVE

When he reflects on the timeline of his business, so much of what O'Connor Fraser did in the past is driving what his company does now and what they look forward to in the future. "I'm not interested in incurring a large overhead," he says. "I now have everything in one room and can do the same amount of work in the same amount of time at even better quality than I could back then. I used to need a full-time editor and engineer but not anymore. Back then you had to invest in gear and people. I had two or three staffers who were making more than a hundred thousand a year, I had middle management, and then I had my salary and Susan's salary."

O'Connor Fraser still shoots, edits and does some writing but he also wears an audio engineer's hat, which he never wore before. "We're trying to find that sweet spot with a core group of five or six people plus freelancers," he said. "I have two ex-employees who handle our 2D graphics and 3D animation. I still have a lot of my people but I don't have to worry about paying them every week. Some of my ex-employees are now clients and they're bringing us a lot of work and that's a bonus."

Technology will continue to have a tremendous impact on the corporate video production industry. That said, you still tend to get what you pay for. You just get more now from Tam Communications. "My daughter swore she would never work for the family business but she is now very much my right hand person," said O'Connor Fraser. "I can't even imagine functioning without her. I had her direct all the big Boardwalk commercials. She's been around the business all her life and has a really good photographic and composition sense and she has directing talent. She's going to be the future of our business. I won't hire someone unless they have that passion for the business."

"Sometimes your dream might take twenty years."

MATTHEW BARNETT
FOUNDER / SENIOR PASTOR
LA DREAM CENTER

As Senior Media Producer for Jubilee Christian Center, I volunteered for two consecutive summers at the Dream Center in Los Angeles. This is a place where God performs daily miracles; volunteers come from all corners of the globe to experience the thrill of servanthood. The brightest of all the shining lights at the Dream Center is Senior Pastor Matthew Barnett who was only 20 years old when he transformed a dilapidated hospital into the most extensive rehab facility, rescue center and community food bank in the country. Real people with real problems somehow find their way to the LA Dream Center, where lives change every day.

IN THE BEGINNING

Pastor Tommy Barnett had already established his credentials and was Senior Pastor of Phoenix First Assembly of God but there came a time when he felt a strong calling to reach out to the hurting and destitute in Los Angeles. Barnett tried his best to convince other pastors to join him in this mission but each time his prospective partners would tour the area, they'd decline the opportunity and scoot back to their home churches. They saw the mission fields of Watts, South Central, Compton, Imperial Courts, Nickerson Gardens and Downtown Los Angeles in person and felt those areas were much too dangerous for their liking. Each prospect told Pastor Barnett that a new church in those neighborhoods would be too big a challenge.

But his dream persisted until Pastor Barnett eventually heard God tell him that his son, Matthew, was the one to send to tackle and fulfill this mission. Despite well-founded concerns for his safety, 20-year old Matthew assumed the role of pastor at tiny Bethel Temple in 1994. "No, I never dreamed of pastoring a church at 20 years of age," said the young Pastor Barnett. "But I arrived in LA and thought I would gather some momentum and everyone would want to be a part of my church. I soon realized that was a broken dream. I lost everything. I had nothing left. I had no staff. They all left me."

Young Pastor Barnett was as down as he'd ever been. He needed to take daily prayer walks to sort things out before he could move forward. "I walked and kept my eyes open and then I saw things that I never saw when my eyes were only focused on success," he said. "I saw pain, homelessness and families that were in need. That day the Lord impressed upon my heart to commit myself to the city of Los Angeles for my entire life, to pick up broken pieces and tell people they could dream again. From that point, I began eliminating the stress of trying to build the perfect church. God said to just start using whatever He gave me to help people."

With dwindling activity in the church and the congregation attendance tumbling, Pastor Barnett had an idea to set up his office on the sidewalk outside and ask neighbors who passed by how he could help them. "We started giving away free bags of food in front of my church building," he said. "Then a person at an apartment building donated to the homeless people who had drug addictions. From there it just began to spiral until we had fourteen new church members from the neighborhood."

As his outreach efforts grew and the church began to revive, Pastor Barnett happened upon the old, vacant Queen of Angels Hospital in nearby Echo Park, smack dab in the middle of Filipino Town. The Franciscan Sisters of the Sacred Heart founded Queen of Angels in 1926 and the facility eventually became the largest teaching hospital west of the Mississippi. The sisters served the poor, the sick and the aging for more than 50 years and, after seeing the facility up close, Pastor Barnett envisioned his father's dream becoming a reality in that historic building. He saw a place to offer God's love to the homeless and addicted, to victims of sex trafficking and domestic violence, to emancipated foster youth and to those who are hungry for food and hope. If it was truly meant to be, though, Pastor Barnett needed a modern day miracle to occur.

By 1996, the hospital was vacant but the property had become a popular venue for commercial, film, music video and remote television productions. This would have been a great setting for many other media projects but, despite receiving much higher offers from several major entertainment companies, the owner embraced Pastor Barnett's vision to convert the facility into a spiritual healing center. "One day we made a $3.9 million bid on the vacant 360,000 square foot hospital," he said. "The

143

Catholic Church sold it to us when they could have sold it to Paramount Studios for $16 million. So, the journey began through failure but I tell people that sometimes what you want has to die in order to rediscover what you're ultimately born to do."

"The Church That Never Sleeps" had found its new home and now plays a starring role in more than 80,000 lives each month.

A NEW FORMULA

What changed Pastor Barnett's life most was deciding that the criteria for success would be solely based on his own faithfulness to the community that his church serves. "If I'm faithful I'm going to be here long enough to find a formula," he said. "That was life changing because I was figuratively dying every week based upon who was there and who wasn't there and I began to think I was the ultimate failure. When I decided I was going to commit myself to the finish line, there was a certain kind of freedom in knowing that not everything had to happen overnight. I got a chance to take a deep breath and fall in love with the city of Los Angeles. I didn't need to work on the five year plan that I was so addicted to. With that five year plan I would have gotten a church with two hundred people and a paid off building, but God had something bigger in His vision of faithfulness. So, that process of committing myself to the finish line allowed me to keep my eyes open to many things I wouldn't have seen before if I had only been focused on immediate success."

WE'RE FOR REAL

The early relationship with the neighborhood residents was extremely fragile because many figured that Pastor Barnett was only planning to orchestrate a massive public relations campaign, take publicity

144

pictures and leave after raising gobs of money from the community. Slick preachers often prey on the downtrodden but Pastor Barnett proved himself as the real deal. "The moment we bought the hospital and stepped out on a limb, we only had a $30,000 yearly income but we made a $3.9 million offer," he said. It became the story in the community that this church had no money but still wanted to buy a hospital to take in homeless people. We took on that challenge and soon after everyone said, these people really are making a big investment into the neighborhood. It has continued for 21 years as we build a greater foundation for the community."

The Dream Center does this through mobile hunger relief and medical programs, residential rehabilitation programs for adults, a shelter for victims of human trafficking, transitional housing and shelter for homeless families, foster care intervention programs, job skills training, life skills, counseling, basic education and Bible studies. "We work to meet people where they're at, to bring them hope and a way off the streets," said Pastor Barnett.

NIGHTS IN HELL

Just a few years ago, Pastor Barnett surprised his staff with the news that he planned to spend a few days and nights on the streets of Skid Row, one of the most dangerous and lawless areas of Los Angeles. Staff members, some of whom had lived on the violent streets of LA, did everything they could to convince him not to risk danger, but this was a vision cast by God. "I spent a few days down there in Skid Row living among rats that were the size of softballs," he recalled. "I saw the Porta-potties that were being used for prostitution and trafficking and the most horrifying acts. While I was down there I saw families and children and said to myself we're never going to allow families to be homeless again. I decided that we were going to start a place for homeless families and we'd register every family that lives down there. After three days I learned something very powerful about vision. Most of my visions are born by walking through the streets of my adopted city. Inspiration is born on a mountain top but the vision is born in the valley. So whenever I get tired or weary I just walk down the street to see the pain of my city. All the vision that we've ever needed is found in the depth and the pain of humanity. Visionaries keep their eyes open, see the need and respond."

That experience on Skid Row led to the Dream Center adding 173 beds for homeless people who were at the end of their lifeline. "Seeing the plight, especially the families and children down there, where pretty much all them would be raped or tormented by drugs in the neighborhood, tore me up inside," said Pastor Barnett. "My experience told me this had to be done. I saw different pockets of homelessness, veterans and scores of people who now found themselves homeless. I learned a lot from being there those nights. That was when the vision was born to create the homeless family floor."

TO THE RESCUE

As the Dream Center became more established, the energy depleting challenges of running such a large organization began to catch up to Pastor Barnett. But he quickly discovered that other men and women of faith would volunteer to speak at mid-week services to help ease the burden. "All these different mentors started coming and pulling for us," said Pastor Barnett. "I started inviting guest speakers to share on Thursday nights, really to keep me going, because I wanted to quit at times. We have four to five speakers per week from other churches and they are the ones who have kept me going all these years. They are the mentorship that kept the ministry strong. These pastors would tell us that we had a lot more going for us than we even realized. There are hundreds of them who came on those Thursday nights, week after week, to support me as a leader. That was a desperate time for me as I tried to figure out how to keep going and those pastors are the very ones who kept me energized."

CALLED TO SERVE

When serving such a large organization, the Operations process becomes extremely critical. The staff must be taught the fundamentals that allow them to build an operation of this size for the long-term. "We learn little things like loving where you're at and where you are going," said Pastor Barnett. "The process teaches you lifelong principles that keep you going and it's been the secret to success at the Dream Center. We learned how to find a need and fill it or find a hurt and heal it. The concepts of 'we get to serve' and the 'Ministry of One' are what govern our lives and keep things going. These principles stand the test of time."

FEAR IS REAL

Running a homeless ministry and a rehab program is not the easiest, nor the safest, job in the world. Because of the world where the disciples came from, it's understandable why threats to the staff are common and how fear does play a part in the daily workings of the Dream Center. "You always need to be aware of what's going on," says Pastor Barnett. "We've had traffickers come in and try to get their girls back so we need to have bodyguards around the girls who have been sex trafficked since they were 14, 15 years of age. It's very dangerous and it's a threat to our own lives. Our workers have to change their names. I learned something years ago that changed my life and it's in the Word of

God, *'Perfect love casts out all fear.'* You can't fear what you choose to love. And we choose to love the things that we fear. So you have to be smart, you've got to make sure you protect your workers. They go door to door and there is a certain kind of confidence and awareness that comes with love but you know it's a little bit dangerous, too. The more confident you get, sometimes you let your guard down. You need to look out for each other and at the same time be relentless and fearless when reaching out to people. But love drives out most of the fear that we carry with us."

SERVANT LEADERSHIP

A project of this magnitude must have a visionary at the top but that leader needs to be balanced by others who embrace practicality. Pastor Barnett is a strong believer in the strength of his staff, especially his core group of determined and focused women. "I think passionate ministry that utilizes women as leaders is very important," he said. "God brought me the four or five women who run the day-to-day operations. They are very detail oriented and I have embraced and depended upon them to tell me how to make things happen. To put form and foundation into that, we've utilized dynamic women who have the mindset of taking people fresh from being saved off the streets and encouraging them to flourish. These ladies have that heart to see someone truly make it, rather than just having a place to stay."

The majority of the Dream Center staff has served under Pastor Barnett for more than a decade and there is definitely a need for a higher level of compassion than in the everyday working world. Pastor Barnett says there's something about getting people outside their own boundaries to serve and love others while conducting outreach together. "We have never lost track of the people we're serving," he says. "It never gets to the point where the programs have become too big or where we don't individually serve. A lot of the mentoring that we do is by serving one another. That's really kept the staff unified and we celebrate the little successes along the way by putting ourselves in a position where we are forced to help the broken-hearted people."

LIVES REDEEMED

Nothing gets built without a plan, a foundation and a structure, especially when it comes to people's lives. Structure is everything, according to the man who continues to build the Dream Center vision. "The structure is the thing that most people hate for the first 30 days," said Pastor Barnett. "Graduation from our program goes up to about 70% after the first thirty days because we immerse them with structure. Five-thirty in the morning wakeup calls with no contacts from friends on the outside. For 30 days there is a blackout period, but once the momentum builds, structure becomes a hit. People start seeing the results of what's happening in their life. That's when they start loving the structure and embracing it, even craving it."

The problem with many addicts is that they have done their own thing for so many years. From the outset, the Dream Center begins to reprogram them to serve, love and give. "Don't be a taker. Be a giver to society," says Pastor Barnett. "Don't be someone who drains the resources of family and friends but contribute and be someone who starts giving back. That's why we call it work therapy and serve therapy, because by nature an addict is a taker. We try to break that down by teaching the nature of a giver and a contributor. The structure allows people the freedom to have fun together and to learn and grow together. You'll never see people smoking cigarettes on the steps of the church and just hoping to get clean. We don't approach it like they're people in rehab; we coach them like a university or a college. We don't call it rehab, we call it discipleship, because we believe we are making modern day Apostle Pauls and Peters. We are raising people up and we expect people to reach new levels."

UNLIKELY PASTOR

After more than two decades of serving the community, there are literally thousands of success stories to relate. It's so hard to select just one but Pastor Barnett did recount the story of a man named Gary, who was homeless for about fifteen years, living under a bridge in LA. "Every day we would try to reach him but nothing would ever work and he just stayed under that bridge," said Pastor Barnett. "I tried everything to help him. I tried to give him money. I tried to encourage him but I couldn't do anything to get him off the street. One day a young volunteer grabbed him by the hand and said, *'Sir, no matter what, you're coming to the Dream Center.'* For fifteen years he had refused to get in line to get his food; he just stayed under the bridge. I thought maybe this guy couldn't change but then I saw the courage of this girl who grabbed him by the hand and forced him to get a meal. From then on, he would get his free food and bring it under the bridge. One day he came up to me said, *'I want to go to your rehab program.'* To be honest with you, I didn't think this 60-year old could do it after living under the bridge for so long. I didn't want to say no so I invited him in. He ended up graduating from our rehab program and from Bible school and now he's one of our staff pastors! Seventy percent of my staff are graduates from our drug and alcohol rehab program and it's guys like that who prove you can change. Oftentimes it's just somebody believing in them enough to force them out of their convenience and get

150

them to a place where they see something they've never seen before. Every day I see him preach and it's been a real inspiration to see what has happened in his life."

REAL PEOPLE

The Dream Center church services are held at the same place where the legendary Amiee Semple McPherson led her amazing revivals in the early 1900s. It might be ancient and creaky but the old building can still generate quite a buzz on church nights. "I think that buzz is there because so many people who are new in the Lord are constantly coming in to the house of God," says Pastor Barnett. "There's not a sense of pretense that we've got it all figured out. I think we all come to a place where we are absolutely broken, where we're absolutely in need of God, so there's no pretense about perfection. When people give on-stage testimonies about being in drive-by shootings and gangs, people stand and clap for them. I think there is a freedom in being vulnerable and open about the fact that we take a risk on risky people. I think that's what drives the excitement; what new miracle is going to come out of the building and what new crazy thing is God about to do in the midst of a world that thinks that people are limited by their circumstances?"

DUPLICATE GOOD

Pastor Barnett says that anybody can do what the Dream Center does. Just duplicate what works; help a kid down the street or adopt a public school. "That's why the Adopt-a-Block program has been the most duplicated in the city of Los Angeles," he says. "We have a vision to adopt a thousand blocks in the neighborhoods. Those things spread like wildfire. When you think about 140 blocks and thirty homes that our volunteers

151

serve every week, that begins to add up. But what really gets me excited is seeing the churches that are now running food programs of their own. God has put us in a position where we're able to serve sixty churches, besides our own, with all the food they need to reach their communities. That's how you multiply yourself and it's non-threatening because any church can do what we're doing in its own unique way in their community. That's been the best thing about it."

LOVING FAMILY

Pastor Barnett's career is well-defined by now but there is a behind-the-scenes element that has helped carry him every step of the way. It shows its friendly and loving face each time he walks in the door of his family's home. "My family is the thing that saved my ministry because we deal with a lot of problems and pain," said Pastor Barnett. "We deal with a lot of brokenness and my family is immersed in the life at the Dream Center. I take my kids to club soccer every week and, while I'm love with the Dream Center, I try to show them there's life outside as well. That's extremely important in the longevity of a calling. It's important to come home and know you have this amazing family to be with, when you're around so many people who don't have a family and so many kids who have been abused by their own family. To realize what you have and the legacy that I had with my father never giving up on me is one of the most profound things I've realized. It's hard to take your family for granted when you're around people every single day who would crave to have just one day with their dad being there for them. My family and home has saved my ministry because I have something to go home to that's safe and comfortable. I know that sounds crazy from such a risk taker and a guy living on the edge of danger but what allows you to be a risk taker is to have something stable and foundational to come home to."

QUIETING THE SKEPTICS

At the outset, most people doubted the motives of Pastor Barnett and "those Christian people" who were moving in to the neighborhood. But soon they started to see people who were in rehab cleaning the streets and picking up trash. "We earned the right to be heard by changing the atmosphere in the community," said Pastor Barnett. "We always say that whoever stays in the neighborhood the longest will win the battle for influence. Liquor stores have come and gone, gang members have come and gone but the church has stayed. One of the things I really thought I had to do when I came to LA was to be relevant. I had to understand the plight of the city to reach the city. I had to have a good sense of what was going on. But God really wants us to be more than just relevant; He wants us to be revolutionary. Revolutionary leaders stay, they build, and their effort becomes the framework of vibrant communities. We saw crime drop about 73% during that period because of the influx of the church and the people serving everyday. It helps drive out the negative elements in the community."

NOT DONE YET

The Dream Center recently opened an entire floor of its campus to take in homeless veterans. That's a dream come true twenty years in the making. "I tell leaders that sometimes your dream might take twenty years," said Pastor Barnett. "These are things we've wanted to do for a long time. The long-term vision is to partner with churches that are already doing great work and immerse the Dream Center into their culture. Today, thousands of individuals, businesses and churches in Los Angeles and around the world have caught the vision of The Dream Center, volunteering and giving as God leads."

More than 100 independent Dream Centers have taken root throughout the United States. The goal is not to franchise the Dream Center, but to partner with local churches to take the foundational heart of the Dream Center and plant it in their city. "Maybe it will be the outreach component of what is already happening in major cities," said Pastor Barnett. "There's different ways to help the Dream Center, including bringing youth groups to serve for a week, a month or a year. Kids can come for two years and get college credit by serving at our Dream Center Leadership School.

There are so many different types of leaders and different ways to lead and hopefully this will register to someone who has been leaning in the direction of compassion ministry and serving and making a difference. We've been here 21 years and we're excited about the future."

"If you're afraid, jump on it and do it anyway."

STEVE PAVLINA
PERSONAL DEVELOPMENT BLOGGER

Steve Pavlina caught my attention with an article he wrote about earning his college degree in an extraordinarily short time frame. He issued a challenge to himself and won hands down. Today he's one of the elite personal development bloggers, with more than 100 million visits to his website. In 2010 he donated his articles to public domain and this chapter is an adaptation of one of them. Steve's life purpose is: to live consciously and courageously; enjoy, increase, and share peace, energy, passion, and abundance; resonate with love and compassion; awaken the great spirits within all of us; and to fully embrace this present moment. Learn from his passion for commitment.

YOU'RE KIDDING, RIGHT?

When Steve Pavlina enrolled in college many years ago, he decided to present himself with the ultimate challenge: to see if he could graduate in only three semesters. Not three years, which would've been an impressive feat in itself. No, three *semesters*! He would sign up for the same classes that students would normally take but, in order to accomplish this goal, he would need to take 30-40 units per semester, three times the average student load. Obviously, he'd need to manage his time extremely well to pull this off. "I began reading everything I could find on time management and putting what I learned into practice," said Pavlina. "I accomplished my goal by graduating with two Bachelor of Science degrees (computer science and mathematics) in just three semesters, without attending summer school. I slept seven to eight hours a night, took care of my routine chores, had a social life and exercised for 30 minutes every morning."

In his final semester, Pavlina even held a full-time job as a game programmer and served as the Vice Chair of the local Association of Computing Machinery (ACM) chapter while taking 37 units of senior-level computer science and math courses. "My classmates added up all the hours for each task and concluded that my weeks must have consisted of about 250 hours," said Pavlina. "I graduated with a 3.9 GPA and also received a special award given to the top computer science student each year. One of my professors later told me that they had an easy time selecting the award recipient once it became clear to them what I was doing."

Paulina said he wasn't considered a gifted child and this was the first time he'd ever done anything this dramatic. But he enjoyed the part about challenging himself. "I didn't have any personal mentors helping me," he said. "I didn't know anyone who'd done this before and I can't recall a single person encouraging me to do it. In fact, most people highly discouraged the idea. This was simply something I decided to do for myself."

Since this feat was so against the norm, Pavlina says he needed to convince the computer science department chair to approve the extra units every semester, and his classmates often assumed he was either cheating, had a twin or was just mentally unstable. "Most of the time I kept quiet about what I was doing, but if someone asked me how many units I was taking, I didn't deny it," said Pavlina. "I was the only student with a two-page class schedule, so it was easy to prove I was telling the truth."

Paulina doesn't relate this story to impress anyone but rather to make you curious about how he did it. He pulled this off by applying time management concepts that are readily available in books and CDs. "The time management habits I learned in college have served me very well in building my business, so I want to share them in the hopes that you'll find them equally valuable," he said. "They allowed me to shave years off my schooling while also giving me about $30,000 to start my business, royalties that I earned in my final semester as a game programmer."

CLARITY IS KEY

Pavlina says the first step is to know exactly what you want and when you want it. "In a Tae Kwon Do studio where I used to train,' he said, "there's a huge sign on the wall that says, *'Your goal is to become a black belt.'* This helps remind the students why they are going through such difficult training. When you work for yourself, it's easy to spend a whole day at your desk and accomplish nothing of value. This almost always happens when you aren't clear about what you're trying to do. In the moments when you regain your awareness, ask yourself, 'What exactly am I trying to accomplish here?' You must know your destination with as much clarity as possible. Make your goals specific and put them in writing. Your goals must be so clear that it would be possible for a stranger to look at your situation objectively and give you an absolute 'yes' or 'no' response about whether you've accomplished each goal or not. If you cannot define your destination precisely, how will you know when you've arrived?"

The ideal period for defining and working on specific goals is ninety days, or the length of one season. In that period of time, Pavlina says you can make dramatic and measurable changes, as long as you set crystal clear goals. "Take a moment to write down a snapshot description of how you want your life to be ninety days from now," he says. "What will your monthly income be? How much will you weigh? Where will you be in your career? What will your relationship be like? Be specific because absolute clarity will give you the edge that will keep you on course."

SET THE TARGET

Just as an airplane on autopilot must make constant corrections to stay on course, Pavlina says you must periodically retarget your goals. Reconnect with your clear, written goals by reading them every morning. Post your financial goals on your walls. "During the mid-90s, I went around my apartment putting up signs in every room that said *'$5,000 per month.'* That was my monthly business income goal at the time," he said. "Because I knew exactly what I wanted, I achieved that goal within a few weeks. I continued setting specific income goals, even amidst occasional setbacks, and found this process very effective. It wasn't just that it helped me focus on what I wanted; perhaps even more important is that it made it easy for me to disregard those things that weren't on the path to my goal.

For example, if you set a goal to earn $10,000 per month, this can help you stop doing those things that will only earn you $5,000 per month."

Pavlina says that if you aren't clear on your goals, you should make that your first priority. Don't waste time going through life being unclear about what you want. "Most people wallow way too long in the state of *'I don't know what to do.'* They wait for some external force to provide them with clarity, never realizing that clarity is self-created," says Pavlina. "Waiting for clarity is like being a sculptor staring at a piece of marble, waiting for the statue within to cast off the unneeded pieces. Don't wait for clarity to spontaneously materialize—grab a chisel and get busy!"

BE FLEXIBLE

There's a key difference between knowing your destination and knowing the path you will take to get there. A typical commercial airplane is off course 90% of the time, yet it almost always arrives at its destination because the pilot knows exactly where the flight is going and makes constant corrections along the way. "You cannot know the exact path to your goal in advance," says Pavlina. "I believe that the real purpose of planning is simply so that you remain convinced that a possible path exists. We've all heard the statistic that 80% of new businesses fail in their first five years, but a far more interesting statistic is that nearly all of the businesses that succeeded did not do so in the original way they had intended. If you look at successful businesses that started with business plans, you will commonly find that their original plans failed miserably and that they only succeeded by trying something else. It is said that no business plan survives contact with the marketplace. I like to say that no plan survives contact with the real world."

Best-selling author and business consultant Stephen Covey often uses the expression, *"Integrity in the moment of choice."* What he means by that is that you should not follow your plans blindly without conscious awareness of your goals. For instance, let's say you're following your plans precisely before an unforeseen opportunity arises. Do you stick to your original plan and miss the opportunity, or do you go after the opportunity and throw yourself off schedule? "This is where you have to reconnect with your goals to decide which is the better course," says Pavlina. "No plan should be followed blindly. As soon as you gain new knowledge that could invalidate the plan, you must exercise integrity in the moment of choice. Sometimes you can reach your goals faster by taking advantage of shortcuts that arise unexpectedly. Other times you should stick to your original plans and avoid minor distractions that would take you further from your goals. Be tight on your goals but flexible on your plans."

Pavlina believes that having a clear goal is far more important than having a clear plan. In school he was very clear about his end goal to graduate college in only three semesters but his plans were in a constant state of flux. "Every day I would be informed of new assignments, projects, or tests, and I had to adapt to this ever-changing sea of activity," he says. "If I tried to make a long-term plan for each semester, it would have been rendered useless within 24 hours."

USE SINGLE HANDLING

Instead of using one of the more elaborate organizing systems, Pavlina stuck with a very basic pen and paper To-Do list. His only organizing tool was a notepad where he wrote down all his assignments and their deadlines. "I didn't worry about doing any advance scheduling or prioritizing," he says. "I would simply select the most pressing item which fit the time I had available. Then I'd complete it and cross it off the list. If I had a 10-hour term paper to write, I would do the whole thing at once instead of breaking it into smaller tasks. I'd usually do large projects on weekends. I'd go to the library in the morning, do the necessary research, and then go back to my dorm room and continue working until the final text was rolling off my printer. It didn't matter how big the project was or how many weeks the professor allowed for it. Once I began an assignment, I would stay with it until it was 100% complete and ready to be turned in."

This simple practice saved him a significant amount of time and allowed him to concentrate deeply on each assignment and to work extremely efficiently. "A lot of time is lost in task switching because you have to re-load the context for each new task," he said. "Single handling minimizes time lost in task switching. When possible I would batch up my assignments in a certain subject area and do them all before switching subjects. So I'd do my math homework until it was all done. Then I'd do all my programming assignments. Then I'd do my general education homework. In this manner I would put my brain into math-mode, programming-mode, writing-mode, or art-mode and remain in that single mode for as long as possible. I believe this habit helped me remain relaxed and unstressed because my mind wasn't cluttered with so many to-do items. It was always just one thing at a time. I could forget about anything that was outside the current context."

FAILURE IS YOUR FRIEND

Most people seem to have an innate fear of failure, but Pavlina says that failure is really your best friend. People who succeed also fail a great deal because they make a lot of attempts. "Babe Ruth held the home run record and the strikeout record at the same time," he said. "There is nothing wrong or shameful in failing. The only regret lies in never making the attempt. So don't be afraid to experiment in your attempts to increase productivity. Sometimes the quickest way to find out if something will work is to jump right in and do it. You can always make adjustments along the way. It's the ready-fire-aim approach and it works a lot better than the more common ready-aim-fire approach. The reason is that after you've fired once, you have actual data with which to adjust your aim. Too many people get bogged down in planning and thinking and never get to the point of action. How many potentially great ideas have you passed up because you got stuck in the state of analysis paralysis (i.e. ready-aim-aim-aim-aim-aim…)?"

We all need to understand that failure is not the opposite of success but an essential part of success. Once you succeed, no one will remember your failures anyway. "Microsoft wasn't the first business venture for Bill Gates and Paul Allen," reminds Pavlina. "Who remembers that their Traf-o-Data business was a flop? Jim Carey was booed off many a stage as a young comedian. We have electric light bulbs because Thomas Edison refused to give up even after 10,000 failed experiments. If the word 'failure' is anathema to you, then reframe it. You either succeed or you have a learning experience."

MAKE IT HAPPEN

Letting go of the fear of failure will serve you well. If you're excited about achieving a particular goal, but you're afraid you might not be able to pull it off, jump on it and do it anyway. Even if you fail in your attempt, you'll learn something valuable and make a better attempt next time. "If you look at people who are successful in business today, you will

162

commonly see that many of them had a string of dismal failures before finally hitting on something that worked, myself included," said Pavlina. "I think most of these people will agree that those early failures were an essential factor in their future successes. My advice to anyone starting a new business is to begin pumping out products or devising services and don't worry about whether they'll be hits. They probably won't be. But you'll learn a lot more by doing than you ever will by thinking."

"When you have that passion, nothing is difficult."

JEFF KLEIN
FOUNDER
J&M PHOTOGRAPHY

I met Jeff Klein at a shoot at a senior living community, the first of many times we would share the "stage" over the next three years. Through a combination of my video and his photography skills, we produced some beautiful marketing pieces: calendars, brochures, websites and an elegant coffee table book. I truly respect Jeff's work ethic, something he discusses in his chapter. His self-deprecating sense of humor makes it easy to work alongside him and, as he winds down his business, I pray that he uses his 50+ years of experience to mentor the next generation of photographers.

PASSION

What is it about shooting a camera that makes it so fun and rewarding? We all like to consider ourselves creative photographers, although most of the stuff we post to Facebook are shots of what we had for lunch or heavily filtered selfies that make us look younger, better looking or goofier than we really are.

But the ones who have shot photos for a living, as Jeff Klein has done, have a true passion and a true calling. "I thought about that probably more than I thought about anything in my life, and I don't think I can explain it," said Klein. "I think it's an inner drive, an inner passion that sweeps into you. I recently heard Henry Winkler, who played Fonz on Happy Days, one of the most successful TV shows in history. He said he knew when he was three years old that he wanted to be an actor and that passion stayed with him his entire life. I think he's in his late 60's now and that passion has never left him. When you have that passion and it's all you want to do, nothing is difficult."

Klein says that each time he'd go for a hike he would haul his camera gear while his friends wondered how, and why, he carried so much equipment. He says he once carried a camera and a heavy tripod along the Cinque Terre in Italy and didn't even think twice about it. "It was about ten miles but I carried the tripod all the way over," he said. "Many people do that hike but not while carrying that amount of gear. It never dawned on me that I just couldn't be without that camera and tripod. That passion is what gives you strength."

WORK ETHIC

Klein would always invest far more time than the typical photographer, in the hopes of capturing the ultimate shot at the ultimate moment. He is an absolute fanatic when it comes to the subject of work ethic, something he says is sorely lacking in the 21st century. "My father was a great man," he said. "He is certainly my hero and a guy who put his head down, went to work and said nobody is going to hand you anything unless you earn it. Those are generational values but my father was leading the pack. For us as a family and for me as a responsible person there was simply no other way. I always believed nobody was ever going to help me out or give me anything. If I want to achieve or obtain, I have to work for it. I don't just believe someone is going to hand it to me. I do pride myself on those things and I think that the real reason is I come from a generation where those things were held in much greater esteem than they are today."

ENTITLEMENT?

Klein says the subject of entitlement is often the topic of conversation with his wife, friends and anybody else who will listen. "I'm fascinated by the change, by how prevalent it is, how widespread," he said. "When I bump into somebody who has what are now called old-fashioned values, I just call them regular values. When you see somebody who works hard, and says Yes, sir and No, ma'am, it's a rarity but it should be more common. I often ask young people who are the 20 and 30-something sons and daughters of my friends if they feel entitled. I get a variety of answers saying it's a different time and they feel that they are entitled to a 'work-life balance.' For some, it's more time on their own, more time off, or higher paychecks. It doesn't make them bad people, but it's interesting."

When Klein was working as an executive at Chevron, he was part of an interview committee for the computer department and that's where he saw the onset of the entitlement mentality. "About 50% of them came with the sense of entitlement that you could just feel," said Klein. "However, I never felt more impressed than when I found people who showed up early and talked about what they had done vs. those who asked about the pay and benefits. Other people would come in and talk about challenges that they had overcome and problems that they had solved and things they wanted to do. I loved seeing that and I'm always impressed when I see it."

BEING AN OWNER

Following a lucrative tenure in the oil industry, the next phase of Klein's career was becoming the owner of his own photography business. It wasn't long before he found that having to fend for himself was a totally different animal. "Yeah, it was much greater than I could ever have imagined," said Klein. "Had I known how big that mental shift really was I probably would never have done it. So thank God I did not know. I managed a large department at Chevron for more than 25 years so I was used to barking orders and having them carried out. When I was working on an oil spill I would talk, people would listen, and we would move quickly. When that shifted to being the owner of a photography company I had no one but my wife who would often say you're not the boss of me. It was a tremendous mental shift from being a cog in a large wheel to being the entire wheel."

Hard work, as he learned from his father, gave Klein the tools to make a successful run as a professional photographer. "I just worked harder," he said. "I'm no genius and I don't possess any brilliant skills like Steve Jobs and the real movers and shakers. I figured I would just outlast, outwork and study harder than everybody. I lived, breathed, ate and slept photography. As I watched TV, I would study the different lighting techniques that were being used in the show. I read books on advanced photography techniques and just figured out I was going to be better than anybody else through hard work, study, practice, repetition, experiments, trial and error and it paid off."

ENCOURAGEMENT

As he continued to grow his photography business, Klein would make it a point not to rest on his previous accomplishments. He would take tremendous responsibility upon himself to not let clients of any size down. That lesson was learned during his time at Chevron. "Two of my bosses handed me a file," he recounted. "One boss said, *'Don't screw it up'* and the other boss said, *'Here you go, Tiger. I'm giving this to my best man.'* That made all the difference in the world. I said to myself, I'm his best man so I better do the best I can to prove him right. I just felt that way on the many jobs that I did. Clients would entrust me with the responsibility to get certain pictures so I made sure to get them because I didn't want to let anyone down. That positive feedback is extremely important."

One excuse Klein has heard quite often over the years was *"This is a terrible time to get into the business, nobody is buying, you won't make it."* He ignored it all. "What I always thought was, perhaps out of ignorance, no one's buying your pictures Mr. Other Photographer," he joked. "I think people will buy mine and I think I'm good and I'm too dumb to know otherwise. So I would charge through. Not too long ago we counted 30 photographers come and go from the art fairs and street fairs and art shows and other exhibits. Meanwhile, we were booming. We were in the top three of all photographers making money selling prints and shooting events. At one point we had about 45 different clients. I think back on those people who said this is a terrible time to get in the business and say I don't think so. If you are good it's probably never a bad time to get into business."

TRAVEL DUTIES

Most people think that photographers travel the world on a constant basis. That's not usually true, but at the level Klein and his wife Melissa worked, that was pretty accurate. "We went all through Vietnam for three weeks, through much of China, through Europe and many terrific places with the purpose of capturing that one photo that would be the next flag over Iwo Jima," said Klein. "Sometimes I have several single snaps of a picture that resulted in thousands of dollars of income. You're always looking for that magic picture, so it's work the entire time, which I think people may not understand. I wish I could say we're traveling around and everything is wonderful and we're having fun, but work is work. There wasn't a day or hour that went by when I didn't worry about the light and the humidity and how to get this shot and not get in trouble or offend people or take the wrong picture or break some social or cultural custom."

One thing that Klein would like to make clear is that, like diamonds, everything in the field of photography is harder than it appears. "Here's a quick fact that may interest you," he pointed out. "The keep-to-delete ratio—how many good pictures you get versus how many crummy ones you end up deleting—is about 100:1. For every good one you get, you've shot 100 others that you worked very hard to get. It's just not good enough to make people reach into their pocket and say, *'Oh, my gosh. Here's my money, I need to have that picture!'* That picture really has to sock them in the face with impact."

Klein points out something else that people don't realize, the extent to which good photographs are made, not taken. "You don't take a photo, you make a photo," he said. "Then, in Photoshop we lighten the darks, darken the lights, enhance the sharpness, take out the grain and do many other operations to make it look like your eye saw it. Or, on the other hand, we try to make an artsy photo like a painter trying to evoke a feeling."

Another quick fact: for every hour of shooting, Klein says to count on working in Photoshop for about fifteen hours. That's where the diligent photographer scans through to find the picture, enhances it to the max, and does what's necessary to make it a money making photo. "It's a tremendous amount of work, with the travel, the set-up and preparation, the protection of the gear, then the sheer cost of the travel, the time, and then hundreds of hours to sort through and process the images," said Klein.

DOING BUSINESS TODAY

Once Klein became an established entity, he was never intimidated by the rapidly growing amount of competition. He actually welcomed the challenge more as the years passed. "I was the one who said ten years ago I'm going to be better than everybody and I'm going to sell prints and I'm going to be the best," he said. "Is there ever a good time to get into any business? My answer is, it depends. I think the problem with photography today would be simply the success and quality of cell phone pictures and the belief that has been propagated by all of the providers. *'Do you want to shoot like a pro? Push this button and the phone takes a picture.'* So there is a prevailing belief that anybody who has a cell phone can be a pro and I have seen the watering down of picture quality. Everybody says, *'I've got a picture just like that'* and whips out their phone. So I give it a giant 'it depends.' It depends on what the business is and what the prevailing tide of the day is. Today, who doesn't have a good 8 mega-pixel camera? So it might actually be a little tougher to be selling prints today."

PROFESSIONAL JEALOUSY?

Because of the proliferation of cell phone cameras, the question might be, is there jealousy on the part of pros who see all the amateurs around them successfully taking great (or good enough) photos? "There sure is, but not by me," said Klein. "I think it's from unsuccessful photographers who would rather waste time complaining than accept personal responsibility for taking better pictures or developing an app. I never think 'these young whippersnappers, it was better in the old days.' No, it doesn't matter if it was better in the old days or not. What matters is what's happening today and how you adapt to it. When I see somebody come up with a new app to improve cell phone photos I'm wildly impressed. I wish I had thought of it, I wish I were that smart and creative to come up with it. I admire those who are."

SOLID MENTORING

Klein says he is humbled and flattered to be called a role model for so many budding photographers and he takes the responsibility seriously. He had his own role models as a kid so he knows how critical they are to professional growth. "This is going to sound silly but my role models were the photographers on the football field," said Klein. "I was so impressed that those guys had the tremendous responsibility to capture that big touchdown play or big catch. In my photography classes, sadly, I was bored with Ansel Adams and Dorothea Lange and Edward Weston, all the great photographers whom I admire so much today. I didn't have the maturity to admire them or understand them then."

Klein was appointed the senior advisor for Facebook's largest photography club and has also been an advisor to many other groups. He taught photography and was a judge for the Northern California High School's photography competitions. "I thought it was a terrific way to give back, a way to help others enjoy the passion that I have enjoyed for so long," he said.

STOKE THE FIRE

To succeed in today's world, Klein says the greatest ingredient is having the passion and the drive when you wake up each morning. "If it's all they want to do, I think they'll be fine because they'll be doing what they love, and if they're good, it will work," he says. "I would advise them that the hours and hours of work are much greater than they think it will be. The pay will probably be lower than they think it will be but if they have that drive there is really no stopping them. I used to wake up in the morning and rush out as fast as I could. I would go to parks and hills and mountains and lakes and any place I could find to shoot, shoot, shoot, then race home and put the card in the computer, look at the pictures, study the settings, think about what changes I could make, hop in the car, go out again and shoot, shoot, shoot and run home to repeat the process. Study, study, study."

During the time he owned his photography business, there was never a day when Klein considered what he was doing as work. "It was pure passion," he says. "If you have that kind of drive then you'll probably be OK. If cell phone photography is taking over, you might want to be the best cell phone photographer, or you may want to shift to something cell phones can't do. For landscape photography, all the pretty scenics that we so often see, cell phones and amateur cameras don't do a bad job but it's a little hard to convince people to pay $300 for a big professional photo that they can get with their phone. With other types of photography like fashion, products and events, you cannot cut corners."

BE THE BEST

Klein's final piece of advice would be to keep your eyes open, look for people who need you and go where they are. "There's an old joke about asking a house painter the cost to paint your house," said Klein. "He gives you a number and you say, what the heck, I can do that myself, because people believe they can paint their house themselves. But if you ask a cabinet maker how much he'll charge to put in a new cabinet, nobody says, *'Oh, I can do that myself,'* because few of us can make a cabinet. So you need to be the cabinet maker kind of photographer and not the house painter kind. Do something that people know they cannot do themselves."

"2005 was the bottom of the pit."

DUFFY JENNINGS
COMMUNICATIONS CONSULTANT
SILICON VALLEY LEADERSHIP GROUP

One of the most thankless jobs in sports is that of Media Relations Director. You straddle the fence between working for the team and for the reporters. Poor Duffy Jennings. He had to deal with the Bay Area media, one of the most voracious in all of the major sports markets. He and our crews had some tense moments as we raced to beat our deadlines while Duffy tried to balance 20 different outlets, each wanting "exclusive" player interviews. He's a lot more relaxed now after those turbulent times—and others even more tumultuous—and his resiliency is to be admired.

WHO'S IN CHARGE?

The San Francisco Giants have captured three World Series championships since 2010 and are once again considered one of the elite Major League Baseball franchises. But there were many years of turmoil and last place attitudes following the 1960s heydays of Mays, McCovey and Marichal—think David Green, Chris Brown, Manny Trillo and the Crazy Crab—before the fun and games resumed in the City by the Bay.

Let's flash back about three decades, when 90-loss seasons were the norm and the revolving door of managers was spinning faster than the lottery wheel. After several less-than-magical seasons in the 1980s, including 1985 under the likable but overmatched manager Jimmy Davenport, the Giants finally began to enjoy a new taste of success. The surge was quick and unexpected but fun, especially for insiders like Duffy Jennings, the Media Relations Director of the franchise. "It was kind of a blur, it happened so fast," said Jennings. "We had come off the 1985 season with 100 losses under Davenport. Being a manager obviously takes many different skills other than just being able to play the game. It also takes leadership and strategy and a lot of kick butt management of big egos and that just wasn't who Jimmy was."

By the end of 1985 things couldn't have been worse in terms of morale. So team owner Bob Lurie went out and hired long-time baseball executive Al Rosen to be the General Manager and the first thing Rosen did was revert to fundamentals, hiring Roger Craig as his manager. "That brought an entirely new approach and enthusiasm, and the funny thing about Roger Craig's style was that he was old school," said Jennings. "It was like going back to what we did on the playgrounds. He brought that kind of basic enthusiasm and he loved the game and had an aptitude for strategy."

HUMM BABY!

By that time Jennings had been working for the Giants for five years and, from a PR perspective, he immediately liked and appreciated the enthusiasm that he saw in the guys Rosen had brought in. "Especially Will Clark, Robby Thompson and Matt Williams and the younger guys," he said. "Clark was that old style give-it-all-you-got kind of player. The team seized upon that with a new approach for fans, capitalizing on Roger's 'Humm Baby' spirit. I remember when he was talking with Al and a focus group. The advertising guy, John Crawford, said, *'So, Al what do you think this team is going to be like and what are the strong points?'* Al specifically said, *'You Gotta Like These Kids.'* And so was born a tagline. Obviously it was great from a public relations perspective for a team that hadn't been to a World Series since 1962."

BACKBREAKING SCHEDULE

When Jennings served as Media Relations Director, his seasons typically began in the middle of February and lasted until the last regular season game. Towards the end, post-season play extended into October. "During that stretch I would only have four to six days off in seven months because I traveled with the team," said Jennings. "In the off-season the schedule was more of a Monday-Friday 9-to-5 as you cleaned up one year and got ready for the next. But during the season it began with my arrival in Scottsdale where I would live for six weeks during Spring Training. I would be at the ballpark at 7:00am and generally leave about 7:00pm. I'd go back to the hotel where I would spend the rest of the evening typing up statistics and notes for the next game."

Armed with a long carriage typewriter—no computers or tablets out of 1 Infinite Loop yet—Jennings's primary responsibilities were to

177

keep track of player performance and update daily statistics. "We would write up two to three pages of media notes, including pitching match-ups and stats to show how they'd done against previous teams," said Jennings. "I added notes on hot players, special game news and promotional stuff. It would take a couple hours to prepare for the next day. Once I arrived at the ballpark I checked in with the manager and coaches, got updates on the rotation and the lineup and any injuries, and then passed that information on to the reporters."

During batting practice, Jennings would be a field liaison between reporters and the team, which was not always the easiest assignment. "If a TV crew wanted to talk to Will Clark, I'd go to him and say, these guys want to spend some time with you off to the side or in the clubhouse," said Jennings. "That was the role during batting practice and pre-game but once the game started my position would be in the press box where I kept score and announced pitching changes and substitutions. I was 100% there to accommodate the media."

BEAT THE CLOCK!

After the game the urgency would escalate as each writer and broadcaster tried to beat his or her deadline. Jennings would be in the clubhouse as the liaison between reporters and players to facilitate interviews, or to prevent them in some cases. "The media guy is in a rock-and-a-hard place situation, trying to accommodate both and, in many cases, it's an adversarial situation," said Jennings. "You become not really a member of the team and not really a member of the press. It takes a lot of diplomacy and communication skills to try to coax people to do interviews and I wasn't always successful. When we were on the road I had to accommodate their local media and it could be difficult, particularly in a high impact media center like New York or Los Angeles. The job is really a multi-faceted role as communicator, facilitator and peacemaker and it didn't always go well. I came really close to getting in a fist fight with Jeffery Leonard one day, when he wouldn't go on a radio program because the host was so obnoxious."

LIMITED FAMILY TIME

During the regular season, a typical day would begin at 8:00am when Jennings would begin preparing for that day's game, field questions for interviews and collect mounds of data up until game time. "I would often leave the park around 11:00pm or midnight and then be back the next morning to do it all over again," he said. "Baseball players typically had their off days on Mondays and Thursdays, either for travel or for a rare off-day at home. But generally I would work a ten-game home stand and go home for Sunday dinner with my family. Then Monday morning I would be back at the airport to be gone for ten days in three cities. There were very few days off, particularly when I was traveling."

When Jennings first joined the Giants in 1981 he had the "luxury" of one assistant plus the travel director. By the time he left in 1993, PR had grown to four departments and sixteen employees, evidence of the growth and marketing of baseball throughout that era. "In the beginning I was doing a lot of writing and preparation to produce hundreds of publications every year, from single flyers for promotional events to a full media guide," said Jennings. "Over time I had a staff to help spread the work load a little bit and eventually had people who could travel in my place so I could take an entire road trip off."

7.1 EARTHQUAKE

The one game that stands out for most Bay Area baseball fans was scheduled for Oct. 17, 1989 at Candlestick Park. There were a record number of media members in attendance for Game 3 of the World Series against the Oakland A's. "Because it was on the West Coast we had media in from all over the world, more than a thousand when you count photographers and crew people and technicians," said Jennings. "You have to find a place for everybody to sit and to have power and information and food. So, it was quite a challenge when fifteen minutes before the first World Series at Candlestick Park in 27 years we had a 7.1 earthquake. It didn't injure anybody at the ballpark but certainly shut it all down. As word came in from the Marina District and the Bay Bridge, we learned that people had died and were badly injured. It was then that baseball took a back seat and the World Series was postponed for ten days."

CHANGE IN COMMAND

Fast forward through the rest of the Bob Lurie era to 1992 when the Giants were put up for sale. The team appeared to be headed out of the Bay Area for St. Petersburg, Florida before Peter McGowan and Walter Shorenstein rescued the club at the 11th hour. New ownership took over in January 1993 and that's when team Vice-President Larry Baer told Jennings that the new bosses were cleaning house. "He asked me to stay on for a couple months to help the new guy get acclimated," said Jennings. "That was a huge turning point in my life. One, I was 45 years old and had never been unemployed. I'd worked for 13 years as a reporter at the San Francisco Chronicle before I went to the Giants. My identity was wrapped around both of those careers and suddenly I had no clue what I was going to do. At the same time I had no concerns whatsoever about finding a job because of my contacts, my vast experience and my reputation."

Jennings was born in San Francisco, attended San Francisco City College and San Francisco State, and worked for the Chronicle and the Giants. His identity was San Francisco. "I figured this was no big deal," he said. "I could have gone to another team but I didn't want to leave the Bay Area. I didn't want to go back to the media side but I thought I could go into companies that sponsored sports or baseball. I had tons of contacts, including Bob Lurie. But it turned out to be quite the opposite for two reasons."

NEWSPAPER PRODIGY

At the age of 21, Jennings was a student at San Francisco State but was already a full-time SF Chronicle reporter. The City Editor gave him the job, contingent on Jennings's pledge to finish school. "By the time I was a senior at SF State in the early '70s, I was already covering some of the biggest stories in San Francisco, including the Zodiac case," said Jennings. "But I was going to journalism classes that were being taught by Chronicle editors and one guy actually even refused to allow me to take his class. He said, *'How can I have you on the college paper when you're already working downtown?'* So I quit school after three years and I didn't understand until years later when I was out of a job, that not having a college degree was hurting me."

NO TAKERS

So, in spite of all the connections and his work history, Jennings could not land a job. He endured two years of job interviews and tried to make ends meet by doing some PR consulting with a handful of businesses

181

that Bob Lurie had invested in. "I helped out on a couple of those early startups but I couldn't find regular employment and by 1995, after two years of scrambling around, it got pretty bad," said Jennings. "I was depressed and frustrated and people kept advising me to open my own business. I had a few clients so I opened up Duffy Jennings & Associates and hung a shingle out as a PR guy."

Things actually went pretty well for a couple years. Jennings landed some big accounts and got back on his feet. "I didn't want to start a real company by hiring people so I pretty much stayed as a solo guy," he said. "In 1998 I got a call from a guy who used to work for Easton Sports who told me he was now working at a tech startup. He said the company was going to sell sporting goods on the Internet and they really needed a PR guy. So I met with the CEO of Sportsite.Com and he offered me a job for considerably less than what I had been making with the Giants. But it was a full-time job with medical benefits and stock so I thought, OK, I'll take a chance. My business list wasn't that great and here was a chance to have some security for my wife and two kids."

PAPER RICHES

Before Jennings began work, the company changed its name to Fogdog.com, one of the early DotCom boomers that had burst into the sporting goods industry. Jennings became their PR person and was on staff when the company went public. "So there was a day I was a millionaire on paper while I was making less than six figures income," said Jennings. "I thought this was amazing, absolutely phenomenal. But before the six month lockout period ended, the company was sold and now I'm out of work again and I never made a nickel. Even worse, I had already exercised some shares on money I never made. I got some relief on later tax returns but I had to pay $100,000 in taxes on money I did not earn."

Jennings was out of work for the next five years but continued to scrape by. "The year 2005 was the bottom of the pit; my gross income was $6,000," he said. "I had a mortgage plus a wife and two kids. It was just the worst possible time of my life and now I'm over 50. Looking back, if I realized and understood what happened to me, I would have taken the severance money and gone back to school. I was seriously unemployed and it got to be some pretty low times. In fact I ended up getting divorced and moved into a little condo and continued trying to find something to do."

Right around this time Duffy connected with his current wife, Bonnie, who lived in Los Gatos. "After a year my landlord doubled my rent and Bonnie said, *'This is silly why don't you just move in?'* So I moved to Los Gatos with no money, no property and no college degree," said Jennings. "Bonnie was phenomenal in terms of getting me back on track. She had a doctorate in education and worked in high-tech and now I'm in Silicon Valley and I don't know anybody. But one thing led to another until I found a job working for the Silicon Valley Leadership Group, which is a nonprofit business that represented a couple hundred companies. I figured that I would meet a ton of people and that's exactly what happened. That's what I've been doing since 2008."

THROW THE RED FLAG

In 2013, Jennings met a gentleman at a coffee shop who had a background in advertising and local publications. He said he wanted to start a magazine featuring weekend getaway destinations plus information about shopping, wineries, hiking and biking. Jennings was intrigued by the idea and said he would take half of the business, do all the editorial content and have his partner manage the advertising and the marketing. But as the first issue was being shipped from the printer, Jennings found out his partner had no money. "That's my own *naivete'* for not knowing that ahead of time," said Jennings. "He wanted to borrow ten dollars for lunch one day and a red flag went up. A week later he asked me for some gas money and I thought, holy crap, I'm stuck for a lot of money. So I got rid of him and bought him out for almost nothing. I found another guy who was really good and we took that on for the next two years. It got to a point where I was billing almost a quarter of a million dollars but, with the overhead, printing, distribution and other operational costs, we couldn't make any money. I was paying him commissions on advertising but I didn't take any money out of it for two years."

Finally, Jennings told his partner that he was done. "I did a lot of writing and met a lot of people in town," he said. "but the idea is to make a little money and I couldn't do it. So I sold it for just about the amount of money that I had put into it. I'd been funding it out of my pocket and now he's paying me off over time and has done an amazing job with it."

SAVE THE BEST FOR LAST

Things have gone very well since Duffy and Bonnie married in 2008; they recently bought their new house in Danville and are feeling comfortable and secure. "Today I'm 68 years old and half retired but I can't imagine not doing something," he said. "I joined the Diablo Country Club and will ease into retirement but I'm not giving up my job with Joint Venture Silicon Valley. I love working for them. It's easy, I work at home, make my own schedule and it pays well. After all these years of struggle, I now enjoy the luxury of having many choices about my time and travel and other things that we want to do as a company."

Jennings says if you're looking for a happy ending to his entrepreneurial story, there is one. "The end of the story is, Bonnie asked me, *'Why don't you go back and finish your degree?'* So in 2009, at the age of 62, I went back to San Francisco State and got my bachelor's degree in journalism. Not for career or work but for personal satisfaction and to keep a long held promise to an old city editor and to set a tone for my children. I'm certainly proud to say that I did it and my whole outlook changed because of that and because of Bonnie."

"I'm a mechanic of the spine and the human body."

DR. CHRIS COLGIN
OWNER
iCHOOSE WELLNESS CENTER

Part of my recent transformation was losing the 30 pounds that had mysteriously found their way onto my belly over the last few years of life. The man who challenged me was Dr. Chris Colgin, my chiropractor, who's now in the wellness business. Believe me, he knows what he's doing. I dropped my weight, lowered my body fat by 6%, dropped my metabolic age by 16 years and feel better than ever. It makes me happy to introduce Dr. Colgin to those of you who might be considering a chiropractic business…or losing a ton of weight. Chris has the roadmap to both.

WRESTLING WITH PAIN

Dr. Chris Colgin and Patriots Quarterback Tom Brady have at least one thing in common: they both attended Serra High School in San Mateo, California. They were also athletes, although it's a safe bet that Brady's on-field successes have been much more closely chronicled. Dr. Colgin says he was a big fan of sports and very active, but his body didn't always seem to cooperate. "For some reason I had a tendency to get myself injured, no matter what sport I did," said Colgin. "I was trying out for the wrestling team when all of a sudden I started feeling something sharp like a dagger in my lower back. Of course, when you're wrestling in practice you're doing all kinds of awkward and stressful things to your body, going into this position or that position. It got to a point when we were doing slam drills my coach yelled, *'Get off the mat! You're not coming back until you get a doctor's note.'* So we talked to some family friends whose parents happened to be bodybuilders. They were really into athletics and they told me to go see this chiropractor in San Carlos."

Dr. Colgin took their advice and visited the chiropractor's office and noticed that the doctor was heavily involved with the San Francisco 49ers and a variety of local athletes. It was clear that he had built up his own professional sports niche. "He was a very big, muscular person so I wasn't quite sure what this guy was going to do to me. But I'm seeing all these names and people saying thanks for keeping me alive so I guess I'm in the right place," said Dr. Colgin. "I got an X-ray and found out I had scoliosis, a really bad curvature of my spine. He explained that it probably happened through the years of jumping out of trees and doing crazy things to my body. He started to work on me and after my first adjustment I just couldn't believe how much better I felt in such a quick period of time. I would take the bus to San Carlos after school three times a week to get my adjustment. It changed my life forever and that's when I made my decision to become a chiropractor."

PAINFUL SETBACK

Dr. Colgin was a only junior in high school and his parents were thrilled that he'd already made plans to pursue a career path. Then life happened; he got into a serious car accident in June, just two months before his senior year. "I was in ICU for three or four days," he said. "I lost my hearing and fractured both bones in my forearm. I was a mess and after I got home it took me a couple of weeks just to regain my balance. But I went right back to getting myself adjusted by the chiropractor and I was already playing football with my buddies by October. I tell people that I was trained to recover and function at optimum level. My body had the opportunity to rehab because I was getting the chiropractic care I needed. That solidified my decision to go into my career field. I wanted to experience chiropractic and also see that someone else who was in a very bad car accident could recover quickly and efficiently rather than just staying in bed all day."

EXTENSIVE TRAINING

Not many of us know the extent of the education that a chiropractor receives. Their training is equally as extensive as that of a medical doctor. "Yeah, it was very intense," said Dr. Colgin. "I went to Palmer College of Chiropractic West, a thirty-six quarter program, with students attending school all year long. In my first quarter I took 32 units and when Christmas time came my brain was fried. From an educational perspective the amount of hours we spend in the classroom and lab is actually more than someone in a Pre-Med program. I had to know anatomy, physiology and neurology just like anyone else in the medical field. I had to know how the body works and I went in front of a board to get my doctorate. It wasn't like I got some kind of online certificate. I went through rigorous written exams and boards to get my license."

GETTING A HEAD START

Opening up your own chiropractic practice may sound daunting but, in Dr. Colgin's case, the best training experience was to learn the business part of it from someone else, primarily to understand how to do billing and run a smooth operation. He did that for about five years before opening his own practice in 2001. "You don't need much to get started," he said. "Honestly, if someone wants to open a practice they only need two things, a chair and an adjustment table. You could actually have less than 600 square feet and run a very successful chiropractic office. I have a bigger office but that's because we provide so many different services here. Every square foot is valuable so if you're not using it you're losing money, you're wasting it."

To run a startup in any field of business, Dr. Colgin advises hiring a consultant who's going to focus on you, the entrepreneur. Anyone who starts their own business will need someone they can rely on for advice and Dr. Colgin has had his own consultants for many years. "My original chiropractor, Dr. Nick Athens, was the one who really got me thinking about foundational healing, teaching my body to heal on its own without drugs or surgery," he said. "I also give credit to my consultant in San Antonio, Dr. Charles Webb of Freedom Practice Coaching. They really helped me out a lot in business and also with how to communicate with clientele. Tiger Woods and every other athlete and high performer has a coach. You've got to be willing to ask for help because you're going to run into challenges; that's part of growing a brand and part of growing into a businessman and entrepreneur. You're going to take your lumps so you may need that person to say I've been there too, this is what you do. You want to surround yourself with like-minded people when you open your business. My wife, Sandi Rocco, told me a few times, *'Chris, if you don't change the finances, I'm going to fire you.'* So I would advise any entrepreneur to surround yourself with people who can guide you to carry out your vision."

BENEFITS OF CHIROPRACTIC

The biggest benefit most of us regular folks enjoy from chiropractic is stress relief. That includes not only the emotional stress that we feel inside from day to day but also the physical stress on the body. Nowadays, the vast majority of people in Silicon Valley are sitting down anywhere from six to thirteen hours per day. Most of those are at work but the other hours are in the car during the long commute. "Whether they're going to work or going home they're always connected, either on iPad or iPhone or something, so you know they're not moving as much," said Dr. Colgin. "I consider myself a mechanic of the spine and the human body. If you're going to wear and tear it, it's going to need a tuneup every now and then. To reduce wear and tear on the body when you're stressed, you're going to need these tuneups a little more often. People don't have to be in pain to come see us. This is a great way to be proactive so they can stay healthy and efficient. In the sports world, athletes are getting adjustments because it allows them to perform better on the field. That's how you have to look at wellness—do you want to wait for something to happen or do you want to be proactive with your health before something happens?"

191

When Dr. Colgin sees evidence of severe stress, he knows his patients are most likely not providing their bodies the proper kind of nutrition. They come home late so they wind up eating a late dinner and then they stay up late to finish work. They wind up not sleeping well and the vicious cycle feeds on itself day by day. "They're so stressed out that they're eating just to stay awake or they're drinking five cups of coffee per day," said Dr. Colgin. "There's a line at Starbucks at 10 in the morning and at 3 in the afternoon and their bodies are completely stressed out because they're not adapting well to their environment. We teach people from a lifestyle perspective that they're in a vicious cycle and we're going to have to break it. We suggest where to begin and provide an outline to do just that."

PREVENTION EQUALS SAVINGS

Dr. Colgin says businesses and employees can work together to solve this growing problem. The most effective incentive in most cases is financial reward. As we all know, the cost of providing health insurance benefits to employees is soaring astronomically. So if an employer is looking for a way to save money, an efficient wellness program is a good place to start. "There are many employees who want to hear doctors speak about health topics, stress relief and things like that to help them stay healthy," said Dr. Colgin. "If an employee decides he's going to take advantage of a company wellness program, we need to show the employer the positive results that the company can benefit from. If that employee is healthier over a period of time, he and the company both save on the insurance costs. As my wife always says, world peace begins at home. Well, guess what, health does too."

CONTINUE TO LEARN

Dr. Colgin could rest on his laurels, fill his schedule with as many patients as possible, and make a great living. Instead, he makes time for continuing education, which means he and Sandi travel often. "I have always been a student and I love going to seminars," he said. "I believe my job is to always be on top of my game, especially when I develop a health plan or strategy with a new client. I always tell them this is what I'm recommending for now but I want you to know that I am a student of my profession and I'm constantly learning new things. I'm always learning and I'll never be content with what's going on. If I can find an easier, less expensive and more efficient way to help you, it's my duty to do that. I don't like to be stagnant. Who wants to be stagnant, especially when you're living in Silicon Valley where technology changes so rapidly? We have people who hack their bodies now, who want to know which foods cause a reaction and which foods are OK. There's technology to help us find out so much information about someone and how they respond to certain foods."

EARLY WARNING SYSTEMS

That's another key to Dr. Colgin's success: his attraction to technology. He could opt for the bare minimum chair and table but he chooses instead to be an early adopter of the latest and greatest tools. One of his more recent finds is the iHeart, a small device that uses pulse wave technology to measure arterial and aortic elasticity in a non-invasive way. "It's important because we want to find something before it becomes a symptom," he said. "We want to be able to look at things and say you've got something coming down the pipeline here. I don't know what, I don't know when, but if we're going to do something about this, I need to see what it is. If there is some arterial stiffening or if you find yourself breathing heavy when you walk up two flights of stairs that's not a good thing. That means there's something that needs to be fixed now, not later. I want to teach people how to take better care of themselves so they don't have to keep coming to see me for issues that they're literally dying for."

BE SELECTIVE

More people are becoming picky eaters and Dr. Colgin says that's a good thing. The proper diet is very important because it's the foundation for everything we do. "You say you are what you eat, but now it's 'We are what the animal eats or we are where the plant comes from or wherever the soil is.' Everything is now foundational," he says. "We have to start with what we're putting into our mouth, what's the quality of it, where does it come from? People need protein but they're eating chicken and beef with sugar injected into it as a preservative and because it helps give it the nice color. I used to wonder why certain people would have an insulin spike when they're only eating chicken. Well, there you go."

So, based on what Dr. Colgin believes and teaches about wellness and nutrition, organic is the proper way to go. "I don't even want to argue," he said. "My mother started reading food labels in the '70s and '80s. I remember her telling me, *'If it says preservatives are in it, you kids aren't having it.'* Of course, that was all the good cereal, the Captain Crunch and the Froot Loops. People always saw us as a healthy family because she took care of our health. If you read a product label and you can't pronounce the ingredients, don't buy it. When it comes to fruit and vegetables, I won't even touch anything that's not organic. I'm very particular because it makes a difference. Am I going to spend a little more money? Yeah, but I'd rather spend it now than spend it later. If a mother wants her kids to lose weight, maybe if she provides good food on the table they will be healthier. You're the teacher at your house just like I'm the teacher at my clinic."

TAKE CARE OF YOU

Define your whys, whats and whos. Why are you in business, what are you trying to offer, what are you trying to change, and who are you trying to encourage, inspire or influence? These are the questions Dr. Colgin frequently asks himself. "You have to live the lifestyle that you're preaching to other people," he says. "Part of it is making time for yourself to get out of town. Some people think that on vacation it's OK to keep your work phone on. That's why you have a vacation, so you can vacate from your place of employment. I shouldn't have to get a phone call; you pay me to take time off so I can relax and be more efficient for the company. That's why doctors make it clear that we need at least three days to have fun and relax because we put a lot of time and effort into helping our clients. We're in their world, taking on their stress, and trying to be that guiding light to get out of the predicament they're in. My wife is a champion in everything she does and keeps me honest and working at my highest level. We're here to inspire our clients and to understand what they're going through, but we're also here to show them if you just do the things that we ask you to do, the possibilities are endless. It's fun seeing people transform that way."

"What put you on top is developed at the bottom."

KURT ROBINSON, ESQ.

FOUNDER

KROB LAW

As KNTV Sports Director, I co-hosted the San Francisco 49ers post-game show with Ronnie Lott, Ken Norton Jr., Gary Plummer, Guy McIntyre and Roger Craig. That's how I met player agent Kurt Robinson, who figured prominently in the professional lives of many NFL players. Kurt was professional but low-key, unlike the flashy agents who stepped on each other's toes while trying to snag the top talent. Kurt made his presence felt through direct contact with players, and was rewarded with word-of-mouth referrals. Kurt's sports law experience is extensive and his story is a lesson for anyone with a passion for the profession.

LEGAL OPTIONS

Kurt Robinson is a graduate of the University of Santa Clara School of Law and says the best thing about the profession he chose is that it gives him access to a wide variety of opportunities. "I'm a trial lawyer," said Robinson. "Sometimes I'm on trial, maybe on trial in a murder case one day. Then I can switch to be a sports agent where I negotiate contracts for athletes. It just gives you access to a lot of different things. Law is pretty broad so you can do many things with that one career and that's why I chose it."

Before he even gets to trial, Robinson typically sets aside six months to a year just to perform the background work on his court cases. The lion's share of that time and effort is spent in preparation, discovery and investigation. Because of that huge investment of time, Robinson says that coming out on the winning side of a jury trial is the highlight of his court duties. "I honestly believe that there is no amount of money that people can compensate you for winning a murder trial," he said. "The sensation you get from that is similar to the one that athletes enjoy after winning a Super Bowl. You are giving somebody something that no amount of money can buy."

And when he loses in court? "We have to accept and go on," he says. "Your goal is to minimize. You can lose a case but sometimes there can be a victory for lessening the time from life imprisonment. So not every loss is a complete loss."

SPORTS LAW

The job of a sports agent is to negotiate employment and endorsement contracts for athletes and be responsible for communications with team owners, managers, coaches and other front office personnel.

Agents are also available to make recommendations concerning their client's off-the-field options. Due to the length and complexity of the deals that are negotiated, most sports agents are attorneys with a background in contract law and are expected to be knowledgeable about finance, business management and financial and risk analysis, in addition to sports.

While Robinson was still at Santa Clara, he attended a post-law symposium to listen to a gentleman named Wayne Cooper, who was there to deliver a presentation on sports law. That speech by his soon-to-be mentor became the impetus for Kurt's long career representing professional athletes. "We became friends and I must have called him a million times," said Robinson. "I'm a busy lawyer with my own practice and I now understand that I was imposing on this guy. I went to his office many times and repeatedly talked to him about law school and sports representation."

By the 1990s, Robinson owned a full Rolodex of clients, many of whom played or coached in the National Football League. Being a sports agent, though, is not always about negotiating and signing fat contracts then running to the bank to cash in your 20% commission. Sometimes you need to put on your public relations hat and perform rumor control for your client, as he often did for Charles Haley. "Charles was the best player I had because he's in the Hall of Fame now," said Robinson. "I don't think he's quite the character that people portray him as. He never got arrested, never really got into any trouble and never got suspended by the league; none of those things that are common today. He had a reputation as a character but he has some bipolar issues and he's doing a great job at controlling them now. Charles is a very interesting guy and one of my most treasured friends."

WORKING DEALS

Agents must be highly motivated, willing to work long hours and possess the ability to multitask because it's common for them to be in negotiations on behalf of several clients at one time. During his heyday, Robinson had tight relationships with a number of the 49ers players but he doesn't feel his relationship with the San Francisco organization was as deep as it was with the Dallas Cowboys. "In the years when we negotiated deals with the Cowboys," he said, "I had more access to the inner circle than I did with the 49ers. I definitely worked with more Dallas players; at the time it was up to ten guys. Jerry Jones (owner of the Cowboys) is a very interesting guy; he's very personal with his players and to some extent the agents. The access he offers you and his Southern hospitality is really tremendous."

There was, indeed, a strong relationship between Robinson and Jones. The relationship was very trusting, except for one faux pas on the part of the agent. "If there was any distrust in the relationship I think it was on my part because I told the Cowboys that I didn't think Charles Haley would play again and then the next week I signed him with the 49ers," admitted Robinson.

The new man in charge of the San Francisco front office at that time was General Manager Bill Walsh, who had recently completed one of the greatest coaching careers in NFL history. For the run-of-the-mill player agent, negotiating with a 3-time Super Bowl champion might have been a daunting and intimidating task. For Robinson, though, the deal was done smoothly. "Walsh was a great guy to deal with," he said. "Bill was the greatest guy you could negotiate with, ever. This gave Charles a reason to come back."

RELATIONSHIPS

We're in a completely different era of sports now and Robinson no longer maintains a strong focus on player agency. Today's athlete expects to receive the huge mega-contract with all the perks, which is all well and good since their playing careers are often cut short by injury. But Robinson says the athletes also have become accustomed to receiving "extras" from their agents. "Money rules the business," he says. "So much money is spent on training and players expect gifts from agents. All the players I represented were direct referrals so I never spent a nickel to recruit a guy. I think I had a different relationship with Charles and Eric Wright, who might not even have had a written contract but when they were billed they paid on time. I don't know if I could do that with today's player."

That's not to say things were always polite and never spirited or never played for high stakes. Even among player agents, the familiar faces were all feverishly working the sidelines, looking to snag new talent to join their stable. Robinson says the best way to describe their personal relationships was cordial but competitive. "I knew Bob Lamonte (the agent for Green Bay Coach Mike Holmgren and Raiders wide receiver Mervyn Fernandez) because everybody in San Jose knew each other. You can say I had a close relationship with him," says Robinson. "But you know, it's kind of BS to say you have a great relationship with guys you're recruiting against. I don't think agents really have a great relationship with each other but they pretend to. I wasn't really competing for guys, so I was able to maintain decent relationships with all of them."

I AM THE GREATEST!

Robinson never knew his biological father so he says he wasn't influenced at all by him. However, there was an ultra-high profile man who became, without a doubt, his number one role model: The Champ, Muhammad Ali. "I went to an autograph show that Ali was at and I lied to the promoter," said Robinson. "I said I was Ali's lawyer and I needed to talk to him. He was my idol and as soon as I saw him I said, 'Mr. Ali, I lied. I just wanted to meet you. I don't want to shake your hand, I don't want anything from you. I just want to tell you that I idolize you and that's all.' Then he asked, *'You don't want a picture with me, you don't want anything?'* I said, 'No I don't want anything.' In those days, Ali had a personal photographer so he later sent me a picture that is now kind of beat up. But you know, his DNA is on this picture somewhere, because he filled out an envelope with his name on it and sent me this picture in the mail."

PLAN AHEAD

Millions of people are starting their own ventures in today's weakened economy, not necessarily out of love for the business world but out of necessity after being laid off or 'aged out' by companies looking to save money. "We are in a different age where 9-to-5ers who don't want to risk guaranteed paychecks are going to be less stable than entrepreneurs," says Robinson. "The opportunities for people who want to work 9-to-5 and grow their own pension are going to be increasingly limited. People with an entrepreneurial spirit will have a huge part to play in the future economy."

For somebody older than 50, it's very hard to find full-time employment in their field and Robinson says those people are beginning to realize that they better come up with a better long term plan. "But I think that's going to be true for the majority of the public in the years to come," he says. "Entrepreneurism is going to be the main option. The days of working 25 years for a company to earn a pension are limited and I don't think the average person can expect that anymore."

Building any business, whether it be a player rep agency or a one person law firm, takes a special entrepreneurial spirit. Your head and heart may be filled with long-term dreams of success but your "paying the price" days are filled with the ups and downs that go with building a strong foundation. "All entrepreneurs have days when they wish they were safe like 9-to-5ers," says Robinson. "A certain breed of people are risk takers and are willing to risk feast versus famine. The entrepreneur mindset is, you can be successful and you can't fail."

DEVELOP A NEW STRATEGY

Robinson's opinion is that our educational system needs to change its focus and foster entrepreneurial strategies. Schools need to teach people to think in more creative ways in order for workers to be less dependent on our traditional economy. "My daughter has surpassed her Dad already," says Robinson. "She went to Harvard Law School and I think going to the East Coast made her tougher and it was better for her career in the long run. She is not even 30 years old and she is working the Michael Jackson trial. Her law career will surpass anything that I will ever do."

If there is one piece of advice Robinson would give to the budding entrepreneur it would be to persevere and then persevere some more. "That's the hardest thing to do, to not give up and to remain optimistic in the face of adversity," he says. "Great lessons come from adversity and lead to success. Whatever put you on top is developed when you're at the bottom. I've been on both sides so I know persevering through the adversity and learning the lessons can make you successful. Adversity is the key to success."

"I show people the switch and help turn it on."

SONNY MELENDREZ
KEYNOTE SPEAKER
SONNY MELENDREZ COMMUNICATIONS

As a kid, I was a big fan of *The Jetsons* cartoon on Saturday mornings. Little did I know that 40 years later I'd be interviewing one of the show's talented voiceover artists. Sonny Melendrez was voted one of the Top 100 radio personalities of all time after his Hall of Fame career. He's one of the most positive individuals you'll ever meet and, despite his impressive credentials, he's as humble as apple pie. Non-profit groups love when Sonny hosts their events and he's helped raise more than $100 million for charity. It's an honor to devote this chapter to one of the greatest business and confidence builders in America.

MAN WITH VISION

People who regularly take time to notice and reflect upon the things they're thankful for experience more positive emotions, feel more alive, sleep better and express more compassion and kindness. This deep gratitude and enthusiasm for living has been the hallmark of the life and career that Sonny Melendrez will be remembered for. Melendrez is one of the most sought after keynote speakers in America following a Hall of Fame career as a radio broadcaster and voiceover artist. He strives to bring joy and hope to people's lives. "When I speak to my audiences I share that my vision of the future has always been positive," says Melendrez. "I always knew what I wanted to do and everything that I've ever set my mind to has come to fruition. I was always under the impression that this happened for everyone but then I realized in the last ten years that it's been about the power of enthusiasm. I realize that it was a God-given talent that I didn't even know I was using. As they say, when the student is ready, the teacher appears. I'm being given all this information and need to do everything I can to spread that joy and this incredible revelation."

THE POPE UP CLOSE

Our relationships with others greatly determine our personal happiness so shouldn't we focus our gratitude on the people we're thankful for rather than on material things? Melendrez illustrated that concept when he recounted a story about speaking at an all-girls Catholic school in San Antonio. That order of nuns also served at the Vatican and Sister Jo said if Sonny was ever in Rome, perhaps they could arrange a visit with the Pope. "Well, I'm going to Rome," said Melendrez. "This was May 1987 and Pope John Paul II was coming to San Antonio in September. Children in Seattle were writing letters to the Pope and I thought that would be a cool thing for the children of San Antonio to do. That night I went to the grand opening of a travel agency along with the National Promotions Director for TWA. He said they were looking to promote a new flight from New York to Rome. I told him we were doing a promotion with the kids and I'd deliver the letters to the Pope but I was looking for a travel partner. So he said, put it together and let's see what we can do."

Melendrez went to his Program Director and said, "We're going to Rome!" Bill Thorman signed off on it and the station did a big promotion and received hundreds of letters from the kids. "TWA gave us the tickets, Archbishop Patrick Flores wrote a letter of introduction to the Vatican, and we had our bases covered," said Melendrez. "Once we got to Rome, we went to the Vatican gift shop and called to introduce ourselves. They didn't know anything about our business. Nothing. But a nun happened to hear my conversation and said, *'I know the American Cardinal. Do you want me to call him?'* The Cardinal called back and said there would be five tickets for tomorrow's appearance. So we're thinking, OK, we're going to be out by the courtyard and we'll look up and see the Pope."

The next morning the traveling duo arrived to pick up their tickets, which were printed in Italian. The Swiss Guard read the ticket, which said, *prima fila.* "Well, we didn't know that *prima fila* means first row," said Melendrez. "So we go into this beautiful auditorium and were maybe twenty feet away from the Pope for almost two and a half hours, and it was the most unbelievable experience I can imagine. It was like being in heaven. The Pope spoke seven languages so one Cardinal after another stood up and introduced his special guests. A German group of nuns sang *Hallelujah, Hallelujah.* A group of young people played *La Bamba* and the Pope was tapping his feet and moving his head. It was incredible. It was so moving when the American Cardinal introduced a group of Hopi

Indians from Arizona, including the chief and all the braves. Oh my gosh, it was like being with the world for two and a half hours."

Afterwards the usher told Sonny and Bill to remain in their seats and soon after, the incredible day reached its zenith. "After everybody left, the Pope came and shook our hands and blessed us," he said. "It was incredible; from the time I met Sister Jo to the time I met the Pope it was literally sixty days. That's the kind of serendipity that has happened all my life. That's why they say you will see it when you believe it. It's almost like you've got this super power for what you need or want to happen. It is just exciting to get up every morning and feel like this; sometimes I don't even want to sleep."

ATTITUDE OF GRATITUDE

Melendrez says the best way to reap the benefits of life is to notice new things you're grateful for every day and to stretch yourself beyond the great blessings immediately in front of you. He says that opening your eyes to more of the world around you will deeply enhance your gratitude. "Being grateful for what you have and where you came from gives you that ability to appreciate every moment of every day," he says. "My father moved his barber shop to a little center on the east side of San Antonio. It wasn't even a full address; it was 908-1/2 Nolan. We lived in half of that building so that we could afford to attend parochial school and college. Back then the tuition to attend St. Michael's School was $5 a month. My mother made my father promise her that their kids would go to Catholic school, so we did."

Melendrez and his brother Rick are grateful for the wonderful spiritual foundation they built at St. Michael's, then at Central Catholic High and eventually at San Antonio College and the University of Texas at

El Paso. "It's funny because I recently saw a cancelled check that my father wrote to my grandfather who I was staying with when I first went to University," recalls Melendrez. "It was for $5. He was sending him $5 a week to pay for my groceries. Eventually I got my own job, got on radio and now I was sending the money back home."

THE BIG BREAK

Like many of his generation, Melendrez would fall asleep with a transistor radio under his pillow. Whenever his favorite DJ would play the Top 10 he'd know the words to all the songs and flood the station with music requests. "I was listening because I wanted to be on the radio and I knew that one day I would," he said. "So I'm listening to the radio when Don Couser said we're going to call President Kennedy and see if we can talk to him. So you hear the White House operator say, *'I'm sorry but the President is very busy right now,'* and they would hang up on him. Well, around that time, I was doing impressions of the President. So I left a message with the DJ and he called back asking for JFK. "I said, *'Ah, Mr. Couser, what can I do for you? I understand that you've been trying to get ahold of me.'* He's laughing and says, *'Who is this?'* And I said, *'I think you should know. You've been calling my office every day.'* Melendrez finally revealed who he was and the DJ said, *'OK, here's what we're going to do tomorrow. You're going to be the President.'* It was unbelievable. He called me every day for two weeks."

HELLO, MR. PRESIDENT

Ironically, it was shortly before JFK visited San Antonio and Melendrez made sure he saw him in person, forging a dentist's note from his mom. "I got out of school and waited for the motorcade," he said.

"Wouldn't you know it, my best friend's mother was there and she asked, *'What are you doing?'* I told her I was waiting for the President. She said *'All the girls will be coming down from the high school, do you want to go with us?'* I said, "Sure!"

When Melendrez arrived, hundreds of Catholic schoolgirls were holding JFK signs, which he thought was cool. "A lot of these girls knew me because I was always performing at school functions," he said. "So now the motorcade comes and it's an open convertible and the President is loving it. He goes *'Hi, hello. Hi, how are you? Hi, nice to meet you. Hi, how are you? Hello.'* One girl got a button off his coat but I got to shake his hand. It was the most incredible thing to see the President and shake his hand. Ironically, it was the day before he went to Dallas, so we were among the last people to shake the hand of the President of the United States. Those kinds of serendipities are just so incredible."

HALL OF FAMER

Also incredible was the radio career that Melendrez forged, showcasing his passion for entertainment and fun. He was twice named Billboard Magazine's "National Radio Personality of the Year" and is in the Rock & Roll Hall of Fame as one of the Top 100 Radio Personalities of All-Time. Melendrez was presented the National Hispanic Radio Personality of the Year Award by Ricardo Montalban and, in 2003, was inducted into the Texas Radio Hall Of Fame. "I was program manager and DJ at some of America's greatest radio stations, including KIIS, KMPC, KFI, KMGG, and KRLA in Los Angeles and KTSA, KTFM, KSMG, and KLUP in San Antonio," said Melendrez. "I'm happy to say that those stations enjoyed stellar ratings and received many public service awards."

Melendrez has blended his array of talents into a lucrative career as a TV host, actor, radio personality, writer, voiceover artist, commercial spokesman and motivational speaker. He has served as a spokesman for Disney, Pepsi, McDonald's, Sears and Sprint. "Some of my most thrilling moments have come as a motivational speaker and master of ceremonies at the White House Hispanic Heritage Awards," he said. "I also hosted the National "Just Say No To Drugs" Rally and the USO's 50th Anniversary Gala in Paris, honoring the late Princess Grace of Monaco."

The most satisfying times in his life are when he can rally people behind a local or national cause. In 1992, Melendrez was named Inc. Magazine's "Socially Responsible Entrepreneur of the Year." In 1979, he was invited to Washington, D.C. to present his idea to create a national children's holiday. Sunshine Day was officially proclaimed and celebrated in all 50 states on August 19th. "We encouraged parents to spend the day with their children, giving them what they most want and need, time and love," said Melendrez.

President Ronald Reagan commended Melendrez for his efforts in the war on drugs and the Department of Justice presented him with the prestigious "Modern Hero Award" for inspiring youth to "Soar In School".

EXTEND A HAND

Melendrez pictures the ladder of success with you in the middle rung with someone pulling you up while you're reaching down to pull someone else up to you. "I've had some pretty amazing mentors along the way," he says. "When I first got into radio we played a weekend show called America's Top 40 and I thought this guy Casey Kasem had the greatest job in the world. He's broadcasting to 450 stations and counts down the top songs and tells these stories. I thought this was unbelievable, what a lucky guy. I thought to myself, OK, if I ever get to LA I'm going to find Casey Kasem. So I get the job at KMPC in Los Angeles, which was the station of the stars. KMPC had more personalities hosting national television shows than any other radio station in America."

Melendrez was hosting a segment on a show called, *Kids Are People Too*. "So I said I'm going to call Casey Kasem," said Melendrez. "It turns out he listened to me on the radio. So we became friends and fans and one day in 1977 he called me to say, *'I'm going on vacation and was wondering if you would sit in for me.'* So I sat at his microphone and counted down the top songs in all the land and broadcast it around the world."

Melendrez says that Kasem was genuinely a giving guy who even recommended him to another mentor you might have heard of, a fellow by the name of Dick Clark. "Dick was looking for a host for another dance show and they needed a pilot," said Melendrez. "Casey recommended me because he couldn't do it. Here were guys who were at the top, yet they saw something in me. I can't tell you how many people have said, *'I see myself in you'*, and I think that's probably the biggest statement you can make when you're mentoring someone. I not only believe in you but I also see myself in you and I'm going to treat you the way someone treated me when I was your age."

WHAT'S UP DOC?

Another mentor was the man of many voices, Mel Blanc, who many recognize as the voice of Bugs Bunny, Elmer Fudd, Sylvester, Tweedy and countless others. "Again, another incredible dream comes true," recalls Melendrez. "An agent called and asked, *'Have you ever thought of doing cartoon work?'* I said absolutely, and two weeks later I had my first job. I'm driving my 1971 Ford Maverick into the Hanna-Barbera Studios, the home of Yogi Bear and all those cartoons that I watched as a kid. I was there to do voices on the second episode of the second season of the Jetsons with the original cast, including Mr. Spacely, who was voiced by Mel Blanc. We would have these hour long parking lot conversations in-between our recordings and he's telling me this and telling me that and showing me how to do these voices."

Melendrez went on to develop a stellar character repertoire outside of the Jetsons. He created many of the sounds for the Gremlins movie, was the voice of Fred the Cockatoo in the 1970s hit series, Baretta, and was the voice of the Parkay Margarine Talking Tub.

NO MORE SELFIES!

During his radio days, Melendrez broadcast from studios that had all the latest and greatest electronics so he's definitely not opposed to technology. However, he does remind us that one of our biggest challenges as a society today is our cell phone, which is controlling lives. "You've got to control technology, otherwise you get caught up in this tornado of texting and everything else that we do with these devices," he says. "The best communication is face to face and next to that is voice to voice. If you can pick up the phone and call someone it's much better that they hear your voice. Many times people will think this is a Facebook moment so I'm going to take a picture of this. You see people taking pictures of food but they're missing out on life. Oh my God, every moment it's like having your own camera crew and you're more concerned about the production than you are of the actual experience."

SELECTIVE MEMORY

When you're living life fully present and not distracted by the latest media craze or engulfed in the cynicism of today's world, you activate and fine tune what Melendrez calls your Selective Memory. "I believe we're not just the age we are, we are every age we ever were," he theorizes. "That doesn't mean that you act as a child or teenager; it means that you have perspective and you can remember those times. I remember driving my very first car and thinking how cool I was. I can literally take myself back to that feeling of incredible gratitude, thanking my lucky stars that I have my own car. Many people have said that my attitude is very childlike and I take it as a compliment because I think children and the elderly have the right perspective."

Melendrez spoke to four hundred college students recently and told them the best advice was to never take yourself too seriously. "You're not your position, you're not your title," he said. "You are what you give and you are where you came from and you should never forget that. In doing so, you can enjoy every moment and see it for what it is."

WE ARE THE WORLD

The City of San Antonio named the Sonny Melendrez Community Center in his honor to say thanks for his community involvement, which spread blessings to disadvantaged youth and families. Those types of programs have always been a priority for Melendrez. "One of the projects I'm most proud of is The Children of the World Project in 1985, when we had 1,500 kids and volunteers record the children's version of *We Are The World*. All the proceeds from the record sales benefited USA for Africa."

THE SWITCH

Melendrez says he understands that the great miracles in his life didn't occur by accident. What excites him more than anything else is that they're there for anyone. "It's like a light switch that you didn't know you had," he says, "and I come over here and say, hey look, see this little switch here? This is what turns on the light. Watch this. And you say, I can't believe this whole time I had this switch. Today, that's what I feel my role is, to show people where the switch is and help them turn it on."

Melendrez continues to impress audiences with his wit and his zest for life. "Sometimes I look at people in their 50s and 60s," he says, "and whenever I say, *'What's up, Doc?'*, they turn into kids again. I do all these voices and they go nuts and I tell them this is because somebody gave me the gift of themselves. And that is the greatest gift you can give."

"Take that first step towards your fears."

ANN VILLAPANDO-CHAVEZ
EXECUTIVE DIRECTOR
PACIFICA SENIOR LIVING

Ann Villapando-Chavez is Executive Director at Pacifica Senior Living. She's been in the senior industry for ten years and her impact on residents and their families is immeasurable. Her credentials shine even brighter when you consider her executive positions with Disney, Procter & Gamble and Gerber. Ann was also responsible for leading the Selecta Ice Cream brand from boutique status to market leadership in the Philippines. Through her experience as a Fortune 500 executive, senior living expert and independent consultant, her greatest entrepreneurial lesson centers on tackling your fears and the unknowns that you'll face in your new venture.

SENIOR LIVING

Assisted living was a relatively new concept two decades ago but it is now the fastest growing long-term care option for America's seniors. It's a challenging field for those who decide to enter it. Caregivers work a thankless job, staff nurses are stretched to the limit, and executive directors are tasked with making corporate budgets glow while still providing affordable care to seniors who are typically on fixed income. Beyond the requirement to make a profit is the need for residents and their families to feel true caring and compassion in what is now Mom or Dad's home.

Enter Ann Villapando-Chavez, who came to the senior industry by a fluke. She was merely researching the industry for a friend who wanted to invest in senior care but wound up being hired on the spot into a field she had no experience in. After a decade of leading three senior living communities, she is now a highly accomplished executive director in a thriving chain of residences. "My experiences from previous companies prepared me for the senior industry," said Villapando-Chavez. "Of all the industries, the seniors are the most underserved market but they're the ones who need the most support and care, compassion, dedication and commitment. Unfortunately, there are many companies or individuals who get into the industry for the money because it is a very lucrative business. There's a lot of growth and everybody's jumping into it at the expense of quality of service."

What Villapando-Chavez brings to the table is her ability to determine the weak points in an organization and professionalize the industry she loves so much. "I want to make sure that the quality is there, that the dedication and attention to detail is paramount," she said. "You don't take anything for granted. You observe the behavior of the residents, monitor their conditions and understand their history. What has happened to them, what is their current situation? I like to set goals with the family to ensure that we deliver care that exceeds expectations and provide support for them through the entire process. The end goal is to make the seniors not only survive but also thrive and live longer. In my experience, the people who come to communities like ours actually tend to live longer and enjoy the remaining years of their lives."

MEASURE OF SUCCESS

Villapando-Chavez chooses not to measure her personal success, but the success of her overall operation. That includes reams of comeback stories about her residents. "I think the biggest accomplishments are in making sure the residents are taken care of to the point that they improve their condition," she said. "I've seen seniors who come to our communities in wheelchairs thinking they'd never be able to walk again, but they do. I've seen hope restored as they learn to live again and experience things they never thought they would. Seeing the joy on their faces and knowing that they're forging new friendships are my favorite accomplishments."

Villapando-Chavez has managed three extremely profitable senior communities and has increased census at every stop. That kind of success keeps the doors open, staff members employed and ownership happy. But, leading a senior community is much more than turning around the business or delivering higher net operating income or exceeding budgets and profit goals. "I think the most important thing is the end result, which is the care that the residents receive," said Villapando-Chavez. "Obviously, a lot goes into that in terms of training the staff, hiring the right people and making sure that they also understand and share your vision for quality of care. They must deliver on the vision and the goals you set for them, which requires patience because you're not dealing with machines; you're dealing with people with different values, characteristics and personalities. It's my job to ensure that we consistently deliver the highest quality of care."

CHALLENGE YOURSELF

Villapando-Chavez has a very curious mind and by the time she graduated from the University of the Philippines, she had already learned that the key to success was challenging her greatest fears. "I always wanted to learn more," she said. "I started my career with SGV, the most respected consulting firm in the Philippines, then broadened my professional skills at Procter & Gamble. That's when I was able to apply what I was passionate about, brand development and marketing. I learned how to develop and launch products and to understand the needs of the consumer, because that's where it all starts. I had the privilege of managing the Tide brand and launching a line extension which brought Tide to its leadership position."

Based on that success, a track record of excellence had been established. Villapando-Chavez launched the Tide line extension in only four months instead of the 18-month target lead-time approved by P&G management in Cincinnati. Her successful run soon caught the attention of Gus Macuja, an executive at Zuellig Distributors, Inc. "He invited me to learn more about distribution and sales and, since that was an area which I wanted to learn more in-depth, I took the opportunity," she said. "When I resigned from Procter & Gamble, the president of P&G Philippines, Jaime Wallace, gave me a piece of advice that I will never forget. He said, *'You have already learned all the marketing principles that you need to learn. Now go and apply them.'* That advice was crucial because it gave me the strength and confidence to move from one industry to another. As long as I remember that the principles are the same, I'm OK. I took that advice to heart and moved confidently to the distribution company and the results there proved that those principles actually work."

After learning the distribution aspect of business, Villapando-Chavez searched her heart for the next learning opportunity. Which area did she want to experience growth in? "I really wanted to know more about manufacturing so there was a chance to learn that at RFM, the third largest food company in the Philippines," she said. "I selected that opportunity over an offer from a multi-national packing company because I was given the reins to manage the entire manufacturing process. At RFM, I was blessed with the opportunity to lead two Strategic Business Units (Selecta Ice Cream and the Non-Meat Division). After launching Selecta and turning around the Non-Meat Division, the Regional Director of Gerber, Clemente Garrucho, invited me to join him in managing Gerber in Asia Pacific. At that time, I didn't want to leave Selecta since it was my "baby". But he said to me, *'You have already launched the product and made the brand successful. No one can take that away from you. Now it's time to apply the same business principles in a different setup.'* That's when I took a regional position where I could apply my knowledge to projects in different countries."

MICKEY MOUSE OPERATION

One of the highest profile companies in the world is Disney and its reputation for quality is challenged only by the likes of Apple, Ritz Carlton and Coca-Cola. For five years, Villapando-Chavez was Disney's Regional Brand Director for Asia-Pacific. From her home base in Hong Kong, she traveled 75% of the time, covering the dynamic region to reinforce and protect one of the world's most recognizable brands. Disney's standards are well documented and the world-class training she received groomed her for any and all future opportunities. "I handled Consumer Products and

221

was elected to the Global Brand Development Council and was also part of the Asia-Pacific Synergy team," she said. "The Synergy team is composed of executives from different divisions, including theatrical, theme parks, publishing and movies. We planned the launch of properties like Winnie the Pooh, Tarzan and Toy Story 2 when the movies were released in Asia-Pacific. Our job was to make launches bigger than they would be if we were working independent of one another."

GLOBAL EXPANSION

Villapando-Chavez's main responsibility was to make sure that when any new consumer products were launched, the integrity of the Disney brand was maintained. "The Consumer Products division of Disney includes many different categories—food, stationery, apparel and fashion accessories—and we worked with 1200 different licensees," she said. "When we launched products or properties in the market they had to all look like they came from one manufacturer even if 1200 licensees created that collection. I protected the brand integrity and made sure that we didn't just slap characters onto the merchandise and ensured that the licensees were trained to the Disney standards of quality and creativity, including merchandising, in-store displays and promotions. Mickey is the biggest. He's the king of Disney."

FIND THE ANSWERS

Talk to any of the motivational speakers who spew leadership advice and almost all of them will point out the importance of finding a mentor. Although it would be great to spend time (and significant money) with the well-known mentors, you don't necessarily need to be connected with Tony Robbins, Les Brown or Dani Johnson. More importantly, your mentor should be someone you respect and feel comfortable learning from. "I learned the real value of mentorship very early in my career," said Villapando-Chavez. "There were a number of mentors who set really high standards. So high that I'd find myself waking up hearing their voices and the challenges that they had put in front of me. I used to hate numbers but I was trained to look at a profit and loss statement as my scorecard, which I enjoyed. I was frequently tested on sales and distribution numbers, which sharpened my mind and kept me on my toes. If I didn't have the answers, I'd find them. The bulk of my time was spent training my mind and testing my determination with every project that was put in front of me."

FACING YOUR GIANTS

The lessons she learned from those high-ranking executives were ingrained in her mind and absorbed into her work style well before she turned 30. Now she's passing them on to her employees and her children. "One of the lessons I'm passing on is to discover your potential, stretch and face your fears," said Villapando-Chavez. "That's exactly what I did as I developed my career. I feared public speaking and could not even stand up in front of a single person to tell a story. I felt like I was sweating blood in front of my colleagues. I also feared sales, which I think is common. I feared technology but I took a VP of Business Development and Marketing job at a high-tech company. I didn't know programming, but I took that job knowing that was where my greatest growth would come from. I like to encourage everyone to take the first step and move towards the direction of their fears. I had many fears but I figured I could either be defeated by them or defeat them head-on. One or the other. I consciously addressed my weaknesses every step of the way and I encourage everyone to do that."

HIT THE BOOKS!

If you look at the library in her house, you'll soon discover that Villapando-Chavez is an avid reader. She's worked under the guidance of genius level leaders in the past but makes it clear that her learning days are far from over. "Reading is crucial to success," she says. "Unfortunately, many people stop reading when they leave school. I think that's when you should be reading more because you don't have teachers around telling you to *'Read this book from Chapter 1 to Chapter 10.'* It's important because those authors become your mentors. You may not be able to meet John Maxwell or Jim Rohn or Zig Ziglar in person but they are great minds that you can learn from. When you pick up a book, imagine that they're in front of you and actually speaking to you and giving you advice. That's the best way to learn from those books. Don't just read them as entertainment or listen to audios to numb your mind with background noise. Literally take what they say to heart and imagine doing exactly what they're saying. Imagine yourself practicing what they're saying because that's the value of their message. That's how you learn—by investing in yourself. Critics say, *'Oh, all these gurus say exactly the same things.'* That's right, they say exactly the same things because those are the common keys to success!"

KINGDOM BLESSINGS

If you were to pick apart the bevy of self-help manuals through the ages, you'd discover that the most successful business and leadership principles in the world are rooted in the Bible. Strangely enough, though, Villapando-Chavez says many Christian business owners hesitate to adopt the prosperity mindset. "Some people are afraid to be rich because they say it's against their principles," she said. "But He is a God of abundance and wants us to be successful. God wants you to focus on His vision. If you've been given a great vision for a business, how is that bad? It's actually very good and I believe we have a moral responsibility to make it happen."

EXPERT GUIDANCE

Considering the level of experience Villapando-Chavez possesses in the senior industry, creating a consulting firm could be a viable option for the future. Although senior-focused companies abound, many of them fail due to poor financial management, inexperience or a failure to adhere to industry standards. The opportunity to train owners and management teams to increase the standard of care is ripe. "Obviously, when you work for a company, there are directions that you don't control because they are the prerogative of the owner or folks in higher positions," she said. "When you work for someone, it's their vision, direction and money. Regardless, I love setting visions for companies and turning them into reality."

INTRAPRENEUR

Considering the next stage of her career, Villapando-Chavez sees extremely promising opportunities for entrepreneurs who like to control the decision making process. "I've considered myself an entrepreneur within the context of the corporations I worked for," she said. "But, I guess you could say that I'm now an *intrapreneur*. I manage the business as if I am the owner and I love doing that. I have the privilege to set the vision, develop strategies and plans, take risks, innovate and build the business. I do this by leveraging other people's resources and that's a lot of fun!"

For Villapando-Chavez, the three most important keys are 1) a sense of ownership; 2) exhibited leadership; and 3) the clarity of vision. "The Bible says *'Where there is no vision, the people perish.'* For me, that is critical," she said. "What do you really want this company to look like?

What do you really want to accomplish? If that is clear in your head, you will find the answers and the pieces of the puzzle will start falling in place. The keys to providing companies and business owners value for their investment is my experience as a business builder and a leader plus my determination, desire, dedication and passion for what I do. Those ingredients, plus the willingness to work extremely hard."

DON'T HESITATE

The key to starting your own company is not learning everything before you fully engage but having the confidence and the courage to take the risk, knowing that when you start, you will begin to learn everything you need to know. "When I jumped to the manufacturing company, I didn't know much but I took the risk and knew exactly what I needed to learn," said Villapando-Chavez. "Sometimes, the fear of not knowing paralyzes people, so they don't take the risk. I see many successful entrepreneurs who just know deep in their hearts that they have a passion for something and they learn as they go. We can't always have 100% knowledge and if you're waiting for that moment, it may never come. You just need to take that first step towards your fear, feed your mind, and you will find the answers. When the student is ready the teacher will appear."

OH, NO. NOT NETWORK MARKETING!

Another field that is growing exponentially, as more people choose to start their own businesses, is network marketing. Villapando-Chavez used to flinch at network marketers and the stories that circulated about them. Pyramids and scams and MLMs, oh my! "Many of the people got excited about the product but didn't properly train themselves on how to approach people," she said. "Therefore, they became really pushy and turned off a lot of people. I worked and trained in traditional Fortune 500 manufacturing and brand companies and asked myself, why would I get involved in network marketing? I don't get involved in things I don't believe in."

There came a day, though, when her *Tita* Angie gave her samples of some well-known, high quality lotions and potions. "These items were really good products," she said. "So, I never really had that fully negative impression of network marketing because of the positive impression from the product. The negative is typically from the way people push products to the consumers."

Villapando-Chavez got reconnected to network marketing after being inspired to face something else she feared: direct sales. "I'd gone through consumer products, financial services, consulting and other industries and I didn't like network marketing," she said. "But, I thought maybe I should get in and study it, just to be fair. I was blessed to rise through the ranks of Arbonne, a personal care company that produces amazing Swiss-based, natural, vegan products. Working with my friend Johti Dietrich resurrected my faith in network marketing."

There are companies out there that create really good products and the best way to get them to market is through word of mouth. Villapando-Chavez says that network marketing, done well, can be a beautiful business in a practical way. "Provided you have the right product, idea or service, it's a good method to get to the consumer," she said. "Here's why: 1) It's very personal as you bond with your consumer. You understand their needs and have a connection. It may only be a one-time connection, but it also could be a forever connection. 2) Once you attach yourself to an awesome company, you receive awesome training and are surrounded by people who inspire you and who truly care for you. They feed you positive messages, encourage you to go past your fears, break down your limiting beliefs, and spur you on to go for what you really want. Confident leaders surround and support you to achieve that."

In the typical 9-to-5 setting, most higher-ups don't train employees as well as they should because they fear for their own jobs. But in the right network marketing environment, you get trained by people who benefit from helping their teammates. "People want you to succeed," she said. "The real successful network marketing companies are invested in the growth of their people through solid training and they offer products that deliver on consumer's needs, desires and wants. I feel blessed to be associated with a company whose aim is to be the most respected name in the industry and everything they do is world class."

NON-TRADITIONAL WORKERS

As the world's economy continues to stutter and workers with full-time jobs fall victim to salary and benefit cutbacks, more of them are beginning to see shreds of hope outside the traditional work structure. Obviously, entrepreneurship is not for everyone but the trend is clear. "There will always be people who work 9-to-5," says Villapando-Chavez. "It's just like when they said paper would be obsolete and it'll all be digital. There will still be paper; in fact, there's even more paper. There will always be 9-to-5ers because that's how most people's mindsets work. However, I would love to see people attempt something different. Can you imagine a world where everyone has his own business? God has planted a unique seed into every single person. If we're able to tap into that seed and bring it to life and make it grow I think we'll create incredible products and even more jobs. If we ignite that fire and encourage people to bring forth the idea that God has planted in their hearts, imagine that world. That would be awesome!"

On a practical level, more and more people are looking for ways to take control of their lives, find freedom and fulfillment, and express themselves. "In every company I've worked for, I've encouraged my colleagues and staff to think of a business idea," she said. "You won't be in a company forever so you might want to start a business. Whenever I have that conversation and people say they're setting up something, that excites me. That's means they're invested in their own growth and passionate about their lives and want to make a significant contribution."

THINKING VS. DOING

The Bible speaks of being doers of the Word. The same principle can be applied when it comes to being doers of a business idea. "It starts with a vision. It starts with a plan. It starts with an intention. It starts with a desire. The real difference is when you take that first step," says Villapando-Chavez. "The real purpose of knowledge is action because what good is knowledge if you don't take action? You may have a wonderful intention but if it doesn't give birth to the business, it's futile. The difference between somebody who's just thinking about the business vs. someone who's taking action is that one person said I'll do it regardless of my fear. I will take that first step, I will borrow that money, I will write that business plan and I will start building. It comes down to that critical decision to start."

DO IT NOW!

Now is the time to start your new business. I know it can be scary. How do you think I feel, writing this book in the hopes that even one of you will buy it? But it's been in my heart to do this for so long, and I believe the time is right as more people like us look for relief from the drudgery of the 9-to-5 work routine.

One of the original self-help book authors was named W. Clement Stone. In the early 1900's he invested $100 into his insurance company and soon turned the business venture into an empire worth hundreds of millions of dollars. Stone emphasized using a "positive mental attitude" to make money, both for himself and for the millions of people who became his disciples through the self-help books and magazines he wrote, edited and published. He was famous for inspiring his employees to recite the phrase, "Do it now!" at the beginning of each workday. He taught that, whenever you feel the tendency towards laziness and know there's something you should be doing, stop and say out loud, "Do it now! Do it now! Do it now!"

DON'T DELAY

There is a tremendous cost in delaying your plans to start a new business because you will mentally revisit them, which can add up to an enormous amount of wasted time. Thinking and planning are important, but action is far more critical. You don't get paid for your thoughts and plans. You only get paid for your results. When in doubt, act boldly, as if it were impossible to fail. In essence, it is.

If a decision can be made right away, make it. Pour the bulk of your time into action, not deciding, because the state of indecision is a

231

major time waster. Make a firm, immediate decision and move from uncertainty to certainty to action. Let the world tell you when you're wrong and you'll soon gain enough experience to make accurate, intelligent decisions that further your goals.

ON WINGS LIKE EAGLES

If you ever get close enough to get a glimpse inside an eagle's nest, you'll see something fascinating. A mother eagle starts building the nest with spiny thorns, broken branches, sharp rocks and other items that seem entirely unsuitable for the project. Then she lines the nest with a thick padding of wool, feathers and fur from animals she has killed, making it soft and comfortable for her chicks.

By the time the growing birds reach flying age, they are reluctant to leave because the soft nest is so comfortable. That's when the mother eagle begins pulling up the soft carpet, exposing the sharp rocks, spiny thorns and broken branches. As more of the soft nest is removed, the bed becomes more uncomfortable for the young eagles. This encourages them to leave their home and graduate to flight school.

In order to move forward, the young eagles must be made uncomfortable. Likewise, in order for us to move forward into career, financial and spiritual maturity, sometimes we need the same thing. Get out of your comfort zone and put yourself in a place where you have to jump out and trust that you will soar!

I wish all of you the best in developing and growing your new businesses. Please keep me posted as you move through the process and maybe you'll be featured in my next book.

HOW BIG IS YOUR DREAM?

PARTNER WITH RICK CHAVEZ

If you would like to partner with Rick on his next entrepreneurial book, or if you'd like to explore ghostwriting options for your own book, feel free to send an email to chavezmedia@gmail.com. Please visit Rick's website at www.rickchavezmedia.com.

www.ingramcontent.com/pod-product-compliance
Lightning Source LLC
Chambersburg PA
CBHW021404170526
45164CB00002B/501